*Graduate Students' Survival Guide*

# Graduate Students'
# Survival Guide

*Ann E. Cambra, Nancy S. Schluntz,*
*Susan A. Cardoza*

McFarland & Company, Inc., Publishers
*Jefferson, N.C., and London*

G
mm

**Library of Congress Cataloging in Publication Data**

Cambra, Ann E., 1947–
  *Graduate students' survival guide.*

  Includes index.
  1. Universities and colleges — United States — Graduate
work. 2. Graduate students — United States. I. Schluntz,
Nancy S., 1944–   . II. Cardoza, Susan A. III. Title.
LB2371.C25  1984      378'.198      83-25610

ISBN 0-89950-112-5 (pbk.)

Manufactured in the United States of America.

McFarland   Box 611   Jefferson NC 28640

*This book is dedicated to past graduate students,*
*as a testimony to their achievement and success.*
*And to current and future graduate students,*
*with the hope our work will turn*
*the mountain into a hill and make the path*
*a little less rocky.*

# Table of Contents

# Acknowledgments

A very special thank you to my husband, Walter Cambra, for his encouragement, sharing, and understanding. He taught me to strive for personal growth and that self-education should be a life-long pursuit. He has been a supportive partner both professionally and personally.

And thanks to Nancy Schluntz, whose editing skills molded the work of three people into a coherent unit.

*aec*

My thanks go first to my family: To my husband, Gregg, who has always encouraged me to set goals and reach further, and lived with me during the growing process. And to my children, Gwen and Sean, who grew up around a procession of "thesis people" and adapted to a business at home as part of family life.

Thanks also go to Ann, who inspired the project and kept it moving, and to Susan, whose creative contribution is not measurable in page numbers. These remarkable friendships survived the book.

*nss*

Special thanks to my husband, Lee Cardoza, for the real spirit of patience he practices with all my projects. I am deeply grateful to my parents, Bill and Alix Haynes, for their help and encouragement

to pursue my goals to contribute literally and artistically. Thanks to
Bonnie Stewart, my beloved aunt, and Edie Duran, my dear friend,
who through the years have counseled me to grow and develop
personally and professionally.

*sac*


Our collective thanks to those who enthusiastically reviewed
the manuscript: Dr. Donald Holtgrieve, professor and graduate
advisor, Environmental Studies Program, California State University, Hayward; Dr. Julia Norton, professor, Statistics Department,
California State University, Hayward; Dr. Derald Wing Sue, clinical psychologist and professor, Educational Psychology Department, California State University, Hayward; and Melinda Shackleford, M.A. (California State University, Hayward) and Ph.D.
candidate (University of California, Los Angeles), who provided the
student perspective. We sincerely appreciate the time spent, particularly in view of their busy schedules, to review and make
valuable suggestions on the manuscript content.

## Chapter 1

# Introduction

In this age of advanced technology, rising costs, shrinking dollars, and stiff competition for jobs, more and more people are obtaining post-graduate degrees. Many of today's graduate students are married, have children, and hold down full- or part-time jobs. These are not ideal conditions for churning out graduate research, but they are becoming an increasingly common fact of life.

With so much of their time occupied with daily survival, students need a helping hand to get through the graduate school experience, including producing a thesis/dissertation. They need more in-depth help than the graduate committee, department or university can supply. Not surprisingly, the book market is flooded with books that give advice on the researching and writing processes; however, we have not found any published source that deals with the specifics of surviving graduate school and processing a thesis/dissertation. We have found a large portion of students with whom we've worked to be unprepared for the parts of the graduate program not included in the university catalog. Departmental politics, personalities of committee members, academic red tape, personal and financial stress make the academic study and research process only a part of the graduate school experience.

From the moment you begin graduate school, you will be faced with questions about procedures to follow, how to tackle the research problem, how to complete your thesis or dissertation. Students have to cope with such questions as: How do I select my graduate committee members? Where do I get a reliable typist? How do I know if my data are analyzed properly? My family life seems to be hurting, can I do something to help it? My committee members just rejected my first draft — does everyone go through this? How do I get everything done if I've moved to another state? It's written ... what do I do now?

This book will provide some answers to these questions, taking you from preparing your program and following university regulations through final submission of the thesis or dissertation to your university. Along the way we'll discuss the academic and personal pitfalls many students encounter that can make pursuing a graduate degree frustrating, confusing, and unrewarding. We'll help prepare you for the unexpected wrinkles that develop just when you thought every possible situation was provided for. Examples based on real experiences illustrate ways to and not to handle a situation. We offer tips on how to get something done efficiently and without being offensive. Dos and don'ts in processing your thesis are discussed.

The book is organized in five major parts, the first being this Introduction. Part II, "Dealing with the Bureaucracy," addresses planning your program, university regulations, and committee selection. Part III, "The Technical Aspects," includes planning your research; editing, writing, and proofreading; typing and word processing; revisions; and graphics and other special typing needs. Part IV, "The Personal Elements," discusses stress, re-entry, your family/friends, your job, grants and other sources of funding, and the post-graduate slump. Part V has the "Conclusions." The "Appendices" (Part VI) include a checklist for your graduate program and tips on preparing your manuscript for typing.

The book draws on our experiences dealing with students — our clients have lived throughout the U.S. and overseas, have been students in major and less well-known colleges and universities, and have been as varied a clientele as is imaginable. If the incidents we have cited seem to touch close to home, it is because we have typed for many students over the years, and all students experience a similar process when going to graduate school. The anecdotes throughout the book are real. However, they have been fictionalized to protect the privacy of the individuals.

Other approaches taken in writing the book reflect our judgment of how to make the information most useful to the reader. For ease of reading we refer to "term" rather than quarter or semester — the time lines are different, but the problems are, for the most part, the same. We also use "thesis" or "manuscript" to apply to either a master's thesis or a doctoral dissertation, unless stated otherwise. Some sections of the book deal with problems specific to each level.

We recommend you read the *Survival Guide* from cover to

cover, then go back and study individual chapters as you need to refer to them. The thought behind this book is that much of the stress graduate students encounter can be overcome by knowing proper procedures, benefiting from experiences of others, and following some basic, common-sense guidelines. This book has been written to accompany you from your entry into graduate school until your thesis or dissertation is safely on the library shelf. Each chapter is meant to be as free-standing as possible within the context of the book. There is, therefore, duplication of some material among the chapters. For example, information on writing technique has not been handled extensively as a separate topic, as there are a wealth of books available on how to write. Rather, we have incorporated specific hints on writing in the context in which they occur (such as how to handle revisions, and how to write in the first place to minimize revisions).

We're not trying to scare you out of graduate school with a collection of horror stories and what-ifs. Some people sail through with no problems. It's not unknown for a thesis to go straight from the student's head to paper and be approved. But many other students, both very organized and downright disheveled, run into problems either beyond their control or of their own making. We want to help you avoid the problems or, if that isn't possible, help you handle them when they come up.

Graduate school can and should be a challenging and rewarding learning experience. By drawing on our collective experiences in working with graduate students and faculty members, some of the burdens can be removed, so *your* energies can go into productive work. The oft-repeated messages are simple:

• Don't be timid, ask questions (of your department staff, your university graduate office employees, your committee members, your typist).

• Advance preparation and foresight can greatly reduce the problems.

• Learn from the experience of others.

• Above all, stay in control of the situation — after all, it is *your* graduate work.

## Chapter 2

# Planning Your Program

Congratulations! You've just been accepted into a graduate program. What do you do now? First, read every available piece of information (catalog description, department handouts). Next, visit the campus. Read the information posted on the department bulletin boards. Meet the department chairperson. Arrange for an appointment with the graduate advisor to plan your course of study and get any additional information about the department and career possibilities. Become acquainted with the department clerical and technical staff (you will find them extremely helpful throughout your program). Arrange for a tour of special department facilities (computer terminal area, laboratories, workshops, testing center, research facilities, special library). Introduce yourself to the faculty members who teach graduate courses.

The important thing in the beginning is to become familiar with the people in your department and the places you will be making use of. *Make your face known* — you want to be more than an I.D. number on a student file!

The actual planning of your program will depend on your field of study and your department. The guidelines offered here are intended to give a general overview of graduate school. Specifics at your university may differ from what is presented here, and portions of this chapter may not apply to your program. However, the material that follows should get you thinking and planning in areas important to the progress of your program.

## *General Department Information*

Once you start attending classes, keep your eyes and ears open.

You will want to familiarize yourself with the general department policy—is it formal or informal, are deadlines firm or are extensions granted, what faculty members espouse the same ideas, do people seem to get along? This type of knowledge will give you insight into how smoothly your program will go, and how to handle problems if they arise.

Equally important, get to know the other students in your department. They can give you invaluable insight into what they have experienced, tips on courses and teachers, help with things like where to get supplies and textbooks at reduced cost, and they may be interested in forming study groups.

Finally, attend all department functions—picnics, luncheons, pizza and beer gatherings, department-sponsored trips to ball games, etc. These are ideal times to get to know your department personnel better, and to participate in the out-of-classroom information exchange that is an important part of any academic experience.

## Acceptance Requirements

Double-check your acceptance letter to find out if any conditions were stipulated for acceptance into the university or your department.

Your status upon entry into graduate school could be as an "unclassified" graduate student—accepted into the university but not yet on a degree track in your department. It may be necessary for you to complete some prerequisites to your major before gaining acceptance into your department.

Departmental acceptance into your program can be on a "conditionally classified" basis. In this instance you are required to meet certain department standards (i.e., maintain a given grade-point average for a specific number of quarters or complete some core courses in your department, which may be upper-class undergraduate courses) before you can become "classified." This is particularly common if you have changed fields from your previous degree or have a marginal G.P.A.

Finally, you can be admitted as a "classified" student into the program. This is admission with no strings attached.

## *Courses*

When you first enter the program, draw up a schedule of courses you plan to take. Then consult with your graduate advisor for approval/alteration. Note the following:

1. Check the university catalog to make sure *all* major requirements are met.

2. Check the university catalog to make sure any non-major requirements are met (i.e., some universities have special requirements *all* graduate students must fulfill, like mathematics or English courses).

3. Make sure the major courses you choose form a coherent program (i.e., you should have a strong core area of related courses giving you special emphasis).

4. Make sure the courses are offered when you plan to take them. (Check the university catalog and verify it at the department office.) If you find a course is not offered when you plan to take it, you may need to (a) rearrange your course schedule, (b) see your graduate advisor about a course substitution, or (c) investigate the possibility of completing the course on your own, under the direction of a faculty member (sometimes called Individual Study). Caution should be used when taking the last approach, however, because you miss out on faculty lectures and class interaction.

5. Independent Study is another option to consider if you want to pursue a course of study in a specific topic not covered in an established course. This involves drawing up a course outline and arranging with a faculty member to supervise your work. Producing your own outline for a course to study is a good way to do preliminary work in an area you're considering for your research project. Don't try this until you are well advanced in the program.

6. Make sure you have prerequisites to courses before you plan to take them. Some universities still have catalogs that list a reasonable number of courses for a degree. But when you look up the courses, you find they may have prerequisites. And when you look up those courses, there are still others that must be taken first. The trick to not losing your way is to map your path carefully and stick to it. A second caution is to pay attention to course numbers listed for prerequisites — don't assume that any related course will meet the requirement. You don't want to waste time taking a second course because the first wasn't the one tailored for business or science or whatever your field of study is.

7. Check to see if there are any new courses being introduced in the department that could enhance your program. Other courses may be recommended, but not required, that would be beneficial in doing your research — statistics, computer, or library study. Squeeze these into your schedule, or set aside time to study them on your own.

8. Most departments offer special topic/seminar courses. These may be required, or just recommended. A seminar course is usually focused on an announced topic, and may consist of a set of five or more meetings during the quarter at which the students present research papers. These papers are not thesis quality, but are more than term papers. If you already know your research project, this work can do double duty by being used as the groundwork or first draft for a chapter in your thesis. Or it might be published as a journal article. The general information in this book is applicable to seminar papers as well as to theses and dissertations — just scale it differently. Another good reason to take seminar courses is for the practice in presenting your research before a group and having to defend it.

9. To go with all this advice to list your courses and take everything you have to or think you need, comes the caution to *not* take courses you don't really need. Courses are very time-consuming and result in a grade. Under the pressure of work at the end or middle of a quarter, it's tempting to let an elective course slide and not do the work because you're taking it "for fun." But the grade still goes on your transcript. If your object is breadth or general knowledge, consider whether you can benefit best from self-directed reading or tutoring rather than committing to a course. Use the telephone and the library. Write letters. A couple of hours spent interviewing an expert can give you more of the information you seek than taking a whole course, and is a more effective way to use the time.

Courses in graduate school are designed to form a unit. By definition, then, they are in some way related. Don't treat them as individual, isolated units of study. Make it a rule to get maximum mileage out of all the work you do. Keep your class notes and copies of all your papers. You may find that much of the work can be used more than once. The reading list prepared for one course can be developed into a paper for another. The paper written for a seminar can become a chapter in your thesis. If you're taking a library research course, choose a possible thesis topic to work on. This double-duty procedure can carry all the way through to post-doctorate work, when the presentation and defense of your dissertation is polished and used as the guest lecture that applicants for faculty positions are invited to give.

## Choosing Your Degree

Careful reading of the graduate catalog, the department handouts and questioning of the graduate advisor in your department will reveal that pursuit of the same basic line of study can lead to more than one degree or concentration within a degree. An M.S. or M.A., thesis or project, can be determined by choice of courses and professors. You don't want to find yourself heading for an M.A. instead of an M.S. because you took French instead of German. Or find yourself short a required course because the section of seminar you took wasn't the one needed for your program. These variations in basic program also affect Ph.D. candidates. However, if you keep your whole plan and goal in mind, individual decisions regarding courses, professors, and research topic will fall into place. Do not hesitate to ask questions of your graduate advisor or department personnel.

There are good reasons for pursuing each course of study. A thesis, for example, is an academic study, whereas a project is an applied study. Work in the arts lends itself better to a project than to a thesis, unless it's an historical study. A project may also be the preferred route for a student who plans to go on to a doctorate, while the thesis may be chosen by someone for whom the masters is the final objective. A thesis is sometimes used as the base document on which the dissertation research is based. If you go directly into a doctoral program from an undergraduate degree, there may be no need to get a masters at all. Or you might want to put the effort into getting a masters in the middle of your doctoral program because it makes a difference in your graduate assistant pay grade.

If you have reasons for choosing a master's degree in addition to a bachelors and a doctorate, consider the field you are pursuing. Obtaining all three degrees in the same field will require you to do double the work in some areas, and perhaps not gain as much breadth as you might like or need. Consider changing fields for at least one of the degrees. One piece of valuable advice offered to undergraduates is to get a broad and solid general education base, and then select an area of specialty. This can be adapted to your graduate career, but must reflect the requirements of your ultimate objective.

One aspect of the quality of a master's degree is the university that grants it. A degree from one university may have higher value than the same degree from another university. There is a tendency of some doctorate-oriented schools to award the masters as an "ABD" (All But Doctorate) degree, or as a booby prize to doctoral candidates who didn't make it. Unfortunately, the single largest sinkhole that doctoral candidates fall into is passing the exams and having nothing left to do but turn in the dissertation, and not doing it. Of those that do not complete the degree, over 50% are lost at this point. If the masters is your final objective, look carefully at the emphasis your university places on the degree.

## Comprehensive Exams

Comprehensive examinations (also affectionately known as CE's or comps) are of two types. The first type is given at about the midpoint of your program to find if you have any deficiencies, and to determine what remedial course work is needed. Although they are anxiety-producing, they should be considered diagnostic. The second type of comprehensive examination occurs at the end of your graduate program, and may be required in addition to or instead of a thesis or dissertation. (Check carefully on the requirements when the exams are in lieu of a written document—it may result in a different degree than the one awarded when the document is submitted.)

Comprehensives are usually written, although some are given orally. A good way to study for them is to draw up questions appropriate to your research and field of interest, and research the answers to them. (Don't forget to cite or refer to all the "greats" on your faculty, especially any on your committee.) Being assertive can be an asset—go to your advisor with your list of exam questions. You may make the professor's work easier, and find that some of the questions appear on your comps. If the professor tosses your questions out, you haven't lost anything and may benefit from your own work in writing them. Other study methods include using departmental study lists, previous exam questions if any are available, and forming a study group with other students in the program. Don't attempt the exams until you have completed enough coursework to get a good background.

## The Research Proposal

Shortly after you have begun your graduate program you will begin selection of your graduate committee (this process is discussed in depth in Chapter 4, "Committee Selection"). The first task you and your committee will undertake is coming to an agreement on what your research will be. This is done through development and acceptance of a thesis or dissertation proposal. In its final form the proposal should provide a clear, detailed, and explicit description of the objectives of your research, the rationale for conducting it, and the methods you will use. It is advisable that the proposal be as detailed as possible, so that it can serve as a skeleton thesis or disser-tation, to be completed by addition of results, discussion and con-clusions.

The basic elements of a research proposal include:

1. *Introduction.* This section should include (a) a clear state-ment of the problem, including its relevance for your field of study; (b) goals of the study; (c) definitions of key terms; and (d) a statement of the theory under study or the hypotheses to be tested.

2. *Background.* This section should be devoted to a review and critical analysis of the relevant theoretical and research literature, and show how your study fits into the cumulative knowledge about the problem area.

3. *Methods and procedures.* Here you tell the reader speci-fically what you intend to do and how you intend to do it.

4. *References.*

5. *Time line.* Estimate the time each phase of the research will take.

Your proposal will be evaluated by your committee members. Once they have agreed to accept it, they and you sign the research proposal contract. Once signed, the contract officially transfers con-tent, method and time line responsibility for your thesis or disser-tation to you and your committee. The signed contract and a copy of the approved proposal will be kept on file in your department office. Be sure to keep a copy of your own! (Refer to Part III of this book for detailed discussion of the steps involved in the research, writing and production of your manuscript.)

## Style Manuals

Before you write your first paper inquire about the manuscript format required by the department. Some fields are very specific about format while others simply ask for neatness and consistency. Style manuals vary in the detail they give, but usually include the basics such as margin width, arrangement of content, and how to cite references. If your department does not specify which manual to use, ask the graduate office which is required for theses or dissertations. If you become accustomed to organizing and writing your papers in the appropriate format early in graduate school, the practice will make working on your thesis or dissertation much easier.

Some commonly-used style manuals are:

William Campbell, Stephen Ballou and Carol Slade, *Form and Style: Thesis, Reports, Term Papers*, 6th ed. (Boston, MA: Houghton Mifflin Company, 1982). About $9.

*MLA Handbook* (New York: Modern Language Association, 1977). About $6.

*Publication Manual of the American Psychological Association*, 2nd ed. (Washington, D.C.: American Psychological Association, 1974). About $12.50.

Kate Turabian, *A Manual for Writers*, 4th ed. (Chicago, IL: University of Chicago Press, 1973). About $4.50.

## Oral Defense

When final approval of your manuscript is near, it's time to make preparations for its oral defense. This includes submitting copies of the *complete* final draft of the document to your committee members, at least two weeks before the date of the orals, so that they can evaluate the work as a whole.

The oral defense allows the student to discuss the research and findings, provides an estimate of the student's ability to respond orally to questions, and gives the committee the opportunity to assess the quality of the research work.

Although you will probably feel a great deal of stress during preparation for and completion of your oral defense, remember that the quality of work put into your research will be reflected. If you have worked closely with your faculty members and have thoroughly understood every aspect of your work (including computer printouts, statistical analysis, etc.), you should have a positive experience — or be able to look back on it as one.

Three different outcomes of the final oral defense are possible:

a. *Unconditional pass.* The committee may consider the candidate's defense satisfactory and the manuscript acceptable as submitted or with minor editing.

b. *Conditional pass.* The committee is satisfied with the candidate's defense, but feels that substantial revisions of the manuscript are required to make it acceptable. The conditions to be met before the degree may be conferred should be clearly specified.

c. *No pass.* This is infrequent, but would happen if the committee were not satisfied with the candidate's presentation or defense, or where major revisions of the document are necessary. If the major conclusions are not supported by the data, or other major but remediable defects are present, a second oral defense may be scheduled when the flaws have been remedied. In some cases failure to pass the oral defense is final, such as when the committee finds the document too deficient to be remedied. Other instances fall under the general heading of unprofessional conduct and include evidence of tampered data, plagiarism, unethical research practices, or unauthorized writing or consultative assistance.

## Time Line

Now that you've explored the basics of planning your program, you have the information needed to construct a time line. Basically, a time line is a series of checkpoints — a tool used to budget time, plan work, and measure success. It's reasonable to construct a time line to cover the length of your graduate program, but be prepared to adjust it when necessary. The greatest tool in formulating a time line is *knowing yourself.* Are you organized? Do you stick to schedules? Are you realistic? Do you perform well under pressure? Do you get discouraged easily? After considering these questions, you should be able to predict whether you need extra time built into your time line to provide a buffer.

The amount of time needed to complete each step depends on the project, but a full-time student could plan on completing the thesis or dissertation by the end of the second year. If you're working, going to school part time, or have a complicated project or one that needs to be conducted seasonally, a three-year time line might be more realistic. Remember that committee members need at least two weeks to read and return written material. Be sure to allow enough time for any bureaucratic delays. In setting up your time line, determine the deadline you want to meet and work backwards from it. You must keep the end date in mind. Make a list of the different stages to be completed and assign estimated completion dates to each stage. Following is a sample of a two-year time line:

*First Year*

| | |
|---|---|
| selection of chairperson | end of fall term |
| committee assembled, first draft of proposal to committee members | end of winter term |
| proposal orals held, proposal approved, contract signed, copy of proposal and original contract to department office. | end of spring term |

*Second Year*

| | |
|---|---|
| first draft of document to committee | end of fall term |
| revised draft to committee | beginning of winter term |
| document in final form to committee | end of winter term |
| final orals and approval of document | beginning of spring term |
| final typing | middle of spring term |
| thesis or dissertation to graduate office and graduation clearance completed | end of spring term |

Thus, by the end of the first program year, the student should have formed a committee, written a proposal, and held orals with committee members that resulted in a signed contract.

By the end of the second year final orals should be out of the way and the final document submitted to the graduate office. The deadline for obtaining thesis or dissertation clearance is at least two weeks before graduation—check this date carefully. To meet this deadline, it is advisable to schedule the final orals meeting at least one month before graduation.

If you are not progressing as quickly as initially expected, update your time line. It is not failure to take more time than planned, and the updated time line will allow you to see your progress. Note in the above sample that time for only one revision of the document was included. If your manuscript is revised extensively more than once, or you are requested to do additional work, the time line will need to be adjusted accordingly. Remember, the end result you are working toward is a completed graduate degree. If it takes longer than anticipated, but the work is eventually finished, you have succeeded.

One last thing to consider when discussing time lines is *stick to your topic*. Keep the research moving and finish your project. Some students tend to run off at tangents, covering unnecessary material and using valuable time in unproductive research. This is especially a problem when the research topic is very broad. The more refined your area of study, the less likely this is to happen. You must control any tendency to explore related areas not in your original research plan. If you are working on a master's thesis and find exciting material unnecessary to your study, it might be a good topic for a journal article or study at the Ph.D. level. Save it for another project!

Some examples of real instances will give you a glimpse of how different students and their situations can be.

Rebecca contacted a typist to schedule delivery of her rough draft the following day. The typist asked the length of the thesis and was told, "I am not sure—it is not written yet. But I will have it finished by tomorrow night to deliver it to you." The typist was astonished! However, Rebecca showed up promptly for her appointment with the completed rough draft in hand. She had worked all night on the thesis, obtained her advisors' approval the next day, and was ready for final typing. [In this case the student knew her advisors were familiar enough with her work to give last-minute approval. Her research was already collected and analyzed, and the literature review had been completed months before. Rebecca believed in her ability to shut out the world for the hours it would take to put everything together and do the writing, and she did it!]

Yolinda completed all her coursework, research, and data analysis, and even had a publisher interested in publishing her final results. However, internal bickering between her committee members so upset the student she finally discontinued work on the project. A friend tried to convince her that "all she had to do was finalize the rough draft" and she would complete the degree; however, Yolinda felt it was not worth the emotional upset she was going through with her committee. [Had Yolinda explored the possibility of changing her committee membership, she might have graduated.]

## Conclusion

The key to completing a graduate degree is planning! It requires getting the necessary information, observing, and writing, as well as complying with administrative procedures. The time spent organizing and updating your time line will be well worth it, because it forces you to analyze your situation, set goals, and think things through. The earlier each step is completed, the easier the process will be for you. It will also flow more smoothly if you get to know the faculty, staff and other students, and participate in departmental functions. Be a live student in the department instead of just a name and number on a file folder — there is a lot more to the graduate school experience than what goes on inside the classroom or research laboratory!

## Dos and Don'ts

Do:

Become a familiar face around your department.
Be sure of any acceptance requirements you must meet.
Make a course plan with your advisor's help; stick to it.
Be sure you are headed toward the degree you had in mind.
Plan a realistic time line, and expect some interruptions in your schedule.

Keep things moving toward completion.

Use your research proposal and time line as working tools.

DON'T:

Get discouraged at setbacks and changes in your time line.

Get bogged down so production stops completely — it might be hard to get started again.

Compare your progress to other students — everyone is different.

Take courses you don't need.

Worry about comprehensives and orals — prepare for them.

# Chapter 3

# University Regulations

The intent of this chapter is to alert you to possible problem areas in dealing with the bureaucracy, and show you where to get questions answered. Dealing with bureaucracies is straightforward *if* you approach it from the right perspective and know when and how to meet the requirements. University bureaucracies have rules, regulations, and more red tape than you can imagine. Failure to follow proper procedures can result in frustration, needless expense, and missing your graduation date. It's a little like driving somewhere on a freeway—you need a general idea of where you're going and how to get there, and rely on the signs only as reminders. If you wait until you see an exit sign to start making a decision, you've missed your turnoff.

Departmental and university politics also play a part in your graduate career, whether you know it—or like it—or not. This topic will be discussed in Chapter 4, "Committee Selection," but deserves mention here. You may be pushed into a research project not of your first choice because your professor needs the backup work for his own research. If you need an extension of deadline date and personal rivalry exists between your committee chairperson and the graduate coordinator, it might be a good idea to ask someone else to request the extension. Likewise, your committee chairperson might be reluctant to ask the department head to bend a rule for you if a promotion or tenure is being considered. These undercurrents of academic life are very real. A professorship is a job, held by a human being who is subject to the strengths and frailties of all humans. Professors don't always leave personal interests at the campus gates. Conflicts of opinion can add healthy perspective to a proceeding, but they may also hamper the cooperative teamwork necessary to keep your program advancing smoothly. Democrats versus Republicans (most strongly during election years), environmentalists versus developers' consultants, men versus women, are common areas of potential conflict, as is the resentment felt for a professor whose outside consulting business is a little too successful.

It's up to you to be aware of what is going on around you and how it might affect your progress through graduate school and the approval of your thesis. The point is to make sure *you* make all possible decisions — not let them be made for you by default.

There are reasons for all the rules and regulations, aside from testing the mettle of graduate candidates. All degrees awarded by a university and theses/dissertations accepted by it are a reflection of its academic merit. It is, therefore, in the university's best interest to set minimum standards. It also helps the staff to do their job better, and should help you know what is expected of you. The rules were not designed to keep you from graduating! In fact, it is possible for the rules to be bent under unique circumstances. Some special options or individually-tailored degree programs do not fit into the mold of established procedures, and administrative personnel have shown remarkable understanding about extending deadlines for students who have demonstrated reliability and competence, but have extenuating circumstances that keep them from submitting on time.

The graduate studies office and your department will have handouts available that explain the necessary information. But you have to question department and university personnel if you are unsure of specific information. It is up to *you* to take the initiative. Keep asking questions until you are satisfied with the answer. It is also a good idea to keep asking the same question of different sources until the answers match!

## Forms and Advancements

As you probably learned when working toward your undergraduate degree, a regular flow of paperwork must be initiated to let the administration know your intentions and progress. *Nothing* happens automatically except submission of grades at the end of each term. The initiator of most of this paperwork is you.

If you were admitted to the university as an *unclassified* graduate student (meeting university admission requirements but either not applying to a specific department or not being accepted by one), you will need to apply or reapply to a department. An acceptance form is sent to the admissions office of the university, and your student file will be sent to the department.

If you were admitted to a department *conditionally*, it probably means you must uphold certain academic standards or take specific courses before the conditions are removed. Another form is necessary to remove the conditional status.

A *classified* graduate student has been admitted to both the university and a department and is on degree track. You can be admitted with classified standing, or you can get there by fulfilling any conditions of admission.

When you have completed enough courses to be ready to take the master's exam, or you have passed the mid-program comprehensives, or whatever the criteria are in your department, you must petition to be *advanced to candidacy*.

After your thesis or dissertation is approved, another set of forms is required. Thesis work will require either a grade in a course for "thesis" or a form *acknowledging approval of thesis*. A dissertation will require a *certification of oral* form and acknowledgment of submission of the document.

Another form that needs to be filed is the *graduation check*. This is a review of your coursework and certification that you have met all the requirements necessary for your degree. Your department completes part of this form and the university records office completes the rest of it. Don't wait until the last possible minute to file the grad check, because it may come back noting that you have yet to meet the general education English requirement or some other out-of-department course required of all students. Or it may note that the appropriate form for some step along the way has not been received, such as certification of completion of orals.

Watch out for the deadline for filing the declaration of intent to graduate and payment of graduation and diploma fees. This may be required two terms or more before your intended graduation date. The *intent to graduate* form should be filed whether you want to go through graduation exercises and receive a diploma or not. The timing on this step is important because it triggers your graduation process. If it takes longer to graduate than you anticipated, you simply file another form. But if you don't file in time, you may find your official graduation delayed. If you do not want to receive a diploma, the university should send you a letter or certificate of completion confirming your graduation and degree. If you do not receive confirmation within the time indicated by the university, check up on it. Also, read your diploma when you get it. It is not uncommon for errors to be made on this last piece of paperwork — wrong name, wrong degree, or omitting any special honors.

Keep track of the paperwork, and keep copies of any forms pertaining to changes in status, acceptance of documents, and payment of fees. Keep your receipts and cancelled checks. Your graduation may be held up because some form didn't make it all the way through the system, and producing your *signed and dated* copy may get things back on track again. Likewise, if admission to a doctoral program or keeping your job is dependent on proof of completion of a master's degree, you may not have the luxury of waiting a year for the paperwork to catch up with itself. (It's better to be a pain in the neck than to be quiet and not graduate!)

Rudolph had been working for a couple of years after completing his Ph.D. He received an offer to teach in a European university, but had to send proof of his degree. When he requested proof from the university he graduated from, he was informed that the proper paperwork had not been completed, and he had never graduated. Rudolph explained that his overseas job offer was contingent upon proof of the degree, but was told the best the university could do would be to grant the degree the following quarter (after he had completed appropriate paperwork and paid fees). Rudolph protested that he had done everything necessary and had his receipts to prove it. Upon producing the receipts and copies of the forms to show he had complied with all regulations, the university granted the degree retroactive to the date on which it had been earned. Rudolph was able to take the overseas job. [To avoid such problems, if you have not received notice of graduation within the time specified by your university, contact them to see if something is holding up your graduation. Keep copies of all your documents and receipts for fees.]

## Thesis/Dissertation Guidelines

Several chapters of this book deal with the writing and processing of your thesis/dissertation, so the topic won't be discussed in depth here. However, one aspect of processing must be pointed out. In the previous chapter ("Planning Your Program") you were encouraged to obtain and start using the style manual preferred by your department. Papers submitted for courses in your department will probably conform to the format used by professional journals in your field. These are usually different in some respects than the requirements for submitting a thesis or dissertation to your university. *When any conflict occurs between university requirements and style manual guidelines, always follow the university requirements.* Failure to do so can result in rejection of the document by the graduate office, even though its content has been approved by the department.

For example, the APA manual was designed for authors submitting papers to professional journals, and is intended to make the typesetter's life easier. It specifies that all material be double-spaced, including tables, in-text quotations, and references. The university will usually specify that these be single-spaced. The manual requires that the location of tables and figures be noted by an instruction:

---

Insert table or figure about here

---

The university regulations are designed to promote consistency in its publications. They will probably require that tables be placed in the text as soon as possible after they are mentioned, or on a separate page immediately following.

University requirements for submission (usually available as a separate handout from the graduate office) will include specific instructions for preparation of the approval and title pages and application for copyright. Other regulations may include:

1. Placing page numbers in specific places.

2. Instructions for making acceptable corrections.

3. Margin requirements. What may appear to be strange margins (2-1/2 inches on the left?) may have been carefully calculated to put the most text on a frame of microfilm.

4. Paper quality will be specified. Some universities even provide a specific list of acceptable brands. Again, there are reasons for this — library-quality paper, which doesn't yellow with age, may be specified if the original typed copy is to be bound for the library.

5. The number of copies needed. You also need to check on the number required by your department, your committee, your parents. It is a good idea to keep one good, unbound personal copy. You may need it to make other copies for binding later, or to rework the format for publication.

6. Destination of the original typed copy — you, the library, or your department.

7. The handout will also give an indication of what the university graduate office personnel check for in a typed document — do they provide quality control over the typing and format, or do they read it and do further editing?

8. Title. Space limitations on the spine of the bound book may restrict the length of your document title.

9. How does the thesis/dissertation get to the bindery and back?

10. The requirements for a master's thesis and a doctoral dissertation from the same university may be very different. Theses may be bound and put on the library shelf, while dissertations are kept on microfilm. Follow the same steps in checking out the requirements for a dissertation as you did for the thesis. This is no time to rest on your laurels!

11. If you are doing a master's project instead of a thesis, your department personnel will probably have final authority. Make sure how their regulations conform to the overall university degree requirements.

These items are to encourage you (1) to be aware that you are dealing with two entities — the department and the university — and (2) to make sure to give your typist *both* the style manual and the university guidelines.

## Conclusions

This is an early version of the refrain you will hear throughout the rest of this book — stay in control of your own program and know what's going on. No administrative process is totally automatic. The best insurance you can get to assure your graduation on time is your own record-keeping and adherence to your planned program.

It is imperative that you obtain all information pertaining to researching, writing, typing, and processing your thesis or dissertation before you actually begin the project. Organizing yourself in advance will save time, money, and frustration. If you still have unanswered questions after reading the information provided by the university and your department, keep asking questions until you get satisfactory answers. The university and departmental personnel, although you may think they sometimes tend to forget it, are there to serve you!

*Dos and Don'ts*

Do:

Keep track of your own program and status.

Obtain a copy of the university catalog and graduate regulations early in your graduate career.

Follow university guidelines when they conflict with instructions in the style manual.

Ask questions of your department staff, the graduate office, your committee members, and your typist.

Determine the due dates and plan your work accordingly.

Ask for an extension if you need one (some universities grant them and others don't).

Don't:

Feel stupid if you have to ask questions — it could save you time and money.

Expect your typist, your committee members and the graduate office staff to bend rules and do the impossible to make up for your being disorganized.

Rush your project — if you need an extra quarter, take it.

Assume anything will be done routinely — keep receipts and make sure forms are filed.

# Chapter 4
# Committee Selection

One of the most important decisions you will make in graduate school, after determining your program requirements, is selection of your committee members (also called "readers"). A unit that works well together will provide guidance during your research and help your thesis come together smoothly. On the other hand, committee members who think along divergent lines can tear you and your project apart at the seams.

Just how important is this committee formation? Consider the following scenario:

Ivy had finished all her graduate courses, completed her research, and had a committee member who was willing to help get the work published. Considerable time had passed since the initial work began. Many changes had been made in her department faculty, leaving only one member of her original committee. When two new members were assigned to her committee, their philosophies differed from the original members'. They were at odds with Ivy and the remaining original member. Result: Ivy was unable to get approval of the work already completed, lost interest in the project, and finally abandoned the work entirely.

Committee selection can greatly influence your schedule and frustration level, and the ease or difficulty of document completion and submission. Given the importance of the committee, the major factors in consideration of potential members are their academic reputation, philosophy, "weight" relative to others, rapport with you and others, and expected degree of active participation in your project.

## *Selecting the Committee*

The time to start your committee selection process is when you enter graduate school or when you are completing your undergraduate work. Observe the faculty members as teachers and communicators. How do they function as members of other students' committees? Can you lay the groundwork and establish rapport with the faculty before it's time to formally set up the committee?

When selecting your committee members, carefully consider these aspects of each potential advisor:

1. Does the person know something about your field of study? This seems obvious, but many committee members do not initially contribute to a student's research. If you are working on your first major research project, you especially need committee members who can help you grow and give valuable guidance in your area. Many students whose graduate work was a bad experience feel their thesis committee gave no guidance, and they lost time and direction.

2. Choose committee members who are familiar with your previous coursework. If a committee member knows the quality of work you produce and likes the way you write, you will have less trouble moving the project from one level to the next.

3. Choose committee members with whom you have a good rapport. You must be able to communicate with them. The fastest road to nowhere follows a breakdown of two-way communication. Sooner or later you are going to learn what they want — better to learn it *before* you've completed the research and submitted the rough draft.

4. Your committee should have good rapport among its members. Your research project is no place for intradepartmental rivalries and politics. Likewise, a faculty member with unique and divergent views may be stimulating in the classroom, but the death knell of a smoothly run thesis project.

Take a moment to reflect on what's been said so far. We are not advocating that students and their committee members (from as few as two to more than six) must agree on everything having to do with the research. You should not get the idea that with a carefully selected committee there will be no disagreement, no changes, no suggestions! However, a committee member unfamiliar with the topic will be of little help in guiding you. And if he or she disagrees with your basic approach you may have to change completely or you will be constantly at odds. If there is disagreement among the committee members your thesis may turn into a battleground, subjected to widely conflicting revisions and directions. What you want is an open, communicative atmosphere where you know what you are doing and where you are going, with the support and aid of your committee. They will want to make changes, suggest new directions, present new ideas so you can explore and grow. This is their function as instructors. But this should be done in the beginning and middle stages — not at the end!

## The Big Name

If you are studying under one of the major "names" in your field, should you ask that person to serve on your committee? There are advantages and disadvantages to weigh, based on the person involved.

*Advantages*: prestige, possible publication, opportunity to learn, employment recommendations.

*Disadvantages*: time constraints on the professor, travel schedule, workload. Keeping track of the professor may be a real strain on you.

The well-known professor has put considerable time and effort into building an academic reputation. He or she may be an up-and-coming young professor with great potential, needing to put many hours into research. Or the professor may be established and have time demands from many areas — the lecture circuit, books, outside consulting. Both will also have their university teaching and research load, in addition to the inevitable administrative duties.

Rex was working on his Ph.D. at a large university. He had one of the biggest names in the field as his committee chairman. Rex had completed all coursework and was in the final stages of writing his dissertation. Unfortunately his committee chairman was in Europe presenting seminars and doing research, so he was unable to contribute to Rex's research efforts. This advisor was simply too burdened with his own professional work to meet the deadlines Rex was facing. Result: The committee member was replaced. Rex had to completely revise the dissertation to incorporate the wishes of the new committee member, but he did finally finish the project.

## Rapport with and among Committee Members

How important is it for your committee members to agree with the type of research you are doing? Students who have produced a thesis or dissertation in which even one committee member did not agree with any portion of the research can attest to the frustration, tears, powerlessness they felt when trying to resolve the situation. Face it: You are at the mercy of your committee when it comes to obtaining their signatures. They say "yes" or "no." If you choose your committee members carefully, they will help you grow and it will be a valuable learning experience. Otherwise, it may be an experience you'll survive, and learn from, but want to forget!

And what difference does it make if your committee members get along with each other? Theoretically it shouldn't make much difference what your committee members think of each other, but in reality it does. If your committee is composed of a close-knit faculty body, you will get the guidance and direction so valued by students. If your committee is composed of warring factions, you will be like the pie sliced up and served as the spoils of war. Sound ridiculous? Look at it from this viewpoint—if you don't get approval (with minor changes) on your first rough draft, or your second, how many times are you willing to submit it? You need the approval of *every* committee member before you are finished.

Amber's project was an historical analysis of the contributions of a prominent local politician. Two of her committee members were of the same political party as her subject, and offered valuable guidance and insight. The other member had been Amber's mentor throughout graduate school. Even though he was of a different political party, Amber felt their established rapport and the professor's academic objectivity would overcome political differences. Not so. The thesis underwent one major revision after another, often with the same paragraphs on drafts bearing conflicting directions from the committee members. The "mentor" finally admitted he had been enthusiastic about the project because he did not believe anything positive could be written about the politician. He had envisioned the thesis as an exposé. The research instead revealed so many positive aspects of the politician's contributions that the professor was unable to bend it to his private beliefs. The situation became worse after the professor was passed over for the chairmanship of the department. After two years of revisions, eight major rewrites, and considerable expense and disillusionment for Amber, her new department chairman finally became involved and replaced the divergent committee member.

Personal prejudice can color your relationship with your committee members and theirs with each other. Even in the theoretically objective academic world, such things as reputation in the community, political preference, personal habits, religion, sex, sexual preference, race, physical handicaps and disabilities, emotional stability, and so forth are very real considerations. You will have to keep your eyes and ears open when evaluating faculty members for your committee. What do students, faculty, and office staff say about working with particular faculty members? Stay alert to what is going on around you. Even if you have no choice about committee membership, this background knowledge will help you establish good rapport and communication with your committee members.

## Hybrid Committees

A project that encompasses several fields of study may require recruiting one or more committee members from outside your department. The most common practice is to recruit one outside member, which may make selection of the second member in your department more difficult than usual. You may also be at a disadvantage in committee selection because of the involvement of the departments themselves.

You can expect members to focus on their own areas of expertise. They may have little understanding or interest in the orientation of the other committee members, and this can lead to obstacles to your progress. But it can work.

Kurt's project required the cooperation of the radio/television and speech/drama departments of one school and the marketing department of another, all within his own university. To his surprise, the faculty members were highly motivated and enthusiastic about his creative approach. They put aside their own differences and worked together to overcome numerous bureaucratic obstacles and help guide his research and complete the project.

Erin's cross-departmental committee took a very different approach.

In Erin's computer analysis of the responses of rats to various stimuli, her biology professors focused their attention entirely on the structure of the research and treatment of the rats. Likewise, the computer science professor regarded the rats only as numbers and focused on the writing of the program and analysis of the data. The project proceeded smoothly in spite of almost total lack of understanding and communication among the committee members.

In cases such as these, the burden is greater on the student to assume an assertive role to assure smooth and steady progress of the project.

## *The Silent Committee Member*

Right about now you are probably thinking a "silent" committee member, one who simply reads the final copy and approves it, sounds pretty good. It sometimes works. But if that silent member decides at the last moment to become an active participant (and it does happen), you will find yourself doing a rewrite after you thought everything was finished. This will cost you time and money.

Earl was working closely with his committee chairman and one other advisor. The third committee member was someone he hardly knew, but who came highly recommended because he was an expert on the topic. This third member agreed to "read" the thesis after it was finished and "sign it off" without really contributing to the research process. After all the work was done and the first two signatures had been obtained, the "silent" committee member read the finished product and wanted major changes made. He had decided if his name was to be on the approval page, then the thesis would need to reflect his standards. Result: Earl revised the thesis, with a great expense of time and money, and finished everything a quarter later than expected. He forfeited a raise in pay for one year because he obtained his degree after the deadline required by his employer.

If a silent member decides to become active, you do have some choices. You can enlist the aid of an outspoken, friendly committee member to help keep the changes to a minimum. Or you can seek to replace the [former] silent member with a new member — and run the risk of changes required by still another person.

It is far better to have an active member right from the start, so you can maintain good rapport through constant feedback, and incorporate all changes before the final typing is done.

## The Assigned Committee Member

What if you have no choice as to committee membership? This can and does happen, especially if you have a very small department, select an area of research that few department members feel qualified to handle or have an interest in, or have a cross-departmental topic. In some universities *all* committee members are assigned, and the student has no choice in the selection. In other cases, the professor(s) of choice may not be able to accept the request because of other teaching/advising commitments. If none of your choices is available, you may wind up with departmentally-assigned committee members. In any of these cases you will have to make the best of the situation. Don't panic! Students have dealt with this situation in the past, and you can too. Here are some recommendations that might help:

1. Try to determine whether your committee members get along with each other.

2. Learn whether the committee members agree on the type of research you should be doing (the direction the research will take) and on the hypotheses you will be testing.

3. Be sure of what you want to achieve.

If you are in luck, answers to the above will be positive. If not, it will be up to you to try to smooth things out. It's not impossible, but it will take more effort on your part.

There are solutions to committee conflicts. One is to select a chairperson from the committee members who can serve as an arbitrator as well as a strong voice for movement forward on the project. An alternative is to suggest that one committee member be dropped in favor of a third party outside your department who is knowledgeable in your research area. (This could be a member of another department, another university, or someone from private industry.)

If you realize a committee conflict exists, you should expect the writing and processing of your thesis/dissertation to take longer than expected (so you may not graduate the quarter/semester you planned). Numerous revisions can also be expected. Knowing these things in advance can save frustration. Ultimately it will be your efforts that keep the project moving ahead.

## Changing Committee Members

Sometimes the membership of even the most carefully constructed graduate committee must be changed. It does happen: professors go on sabbatical, they have babies, they go on leave of absence, they change jobs, they get sick, they retire, they die. In short, your committee members are human.

Bridget, a foreign student, had almost an ideal graduate experience. Her committee members were compatible and her doctoral research was going smoothly. Then, after the first draft was tentatively approved and revisions were under way, her major professor had a stroke. Everything ground to a halt. The professor was incapacitated, but her department's regulations did not provide for replacement of a committee member in event of a temporary disability. In limbo, waiting to see if her professor would recover or not, Bridget's student visa and grant money were running out. After six months of pleading and negotiation, another committee member was selected, but the new committee member required that substantial revisions be made.

If you find you have to replace a committee member, it is not the end of the world, although it may delay your graduation. When selecting a new member, go through the process you used to form the initial committee and things should go relatively smoothly. In addition, seek the counsel of your committee chairperson. He or she may suggest a replacement who would fit in well with the others.

## Involvement of the Department

Your university department may be totally uninvolved in your research project, or it may turn out to be a fourth unofficial committee member. It is to your advantage to find out the extent of the role your department will play. Find out answers to these questions:

1. Is your department chairperson an *ex oficio* member of your thesis committee?

2. Can the chairperson be relied upon to act as your advocate if you have problems with your committee?

3. Does your department have a program of research topics your work must fit into?

4. Does the department read the documents and suggest changes?

5. Does the department have an established thesis review committee independent of your own committee?

6. Which has final authority in your department — your committee or your department chairperson?

7. Does your department have time restrictions for completing a research project which are different from your university's?

8. Does your department require a file copy of your finished document? Bound or unbound?

Your department personnel can provide assistance for you and be a reliable backup if you need it, or they can be another hurdle. You just need to find out which.

## Conclusion

After you've gone to the trouble to select your committee members, use them. Seek advice from them throughout your project. Keep them involved in the work. Make use of their knowledge and experience to advance your research and enhance your educational program. Don't be timid in claiming time from your advisors — that's what they're there for, although sometimes they forget it. If you insist on regular, two-way communication, you will be able to avoid some of the last-stage changes and revisions. (For more about revisions, see Chapter 9.)

Above all, do not forget it is your project. You must take the initiative and be assertive (without being pushy) to keep it moving. If you are aware of your own deadlines and plan your research and writing, you will be able to keep your project and manuscript from bogging down and being buried on a professor's desk.

## Dos and Don'ts

Do:

Pay attention to what goes on in your department — you will hear about potential problem areas.

Select professors knowledgeable about your field.

Select professors familiar with your previous work and who agree with your basic thinking.

Select professors who get along well with each other.

Solicit advice from your committee members.

Keep a log or written record of your meetings, questions, and answers.

Remember, many students have problems with their committee members — and they survived!

Make the best of the situation if you have no choice in committee membership.

Carefully select the committee leader who will best work as a mediator and advocate to move the project ahead.

Be assertive.

DON'T:

Recruit any "big name" professors to your committee unless you are sure they will have the time to spend.

Rely on a "silent" member to make things go easy.

Expect your committee to rubber-stamp what you write; they *will* make changes and suggestions.

Get discouraged because changes are suggested by your committee members — that's part of their job.

Panic if your committee membership has to be changed.

Lose control of your work — it must keep moving forward.

Get your proposal approved and then disappear, to return a year later with a manuscript. Stay in touch.

Chapter 5

# Planning Your Research

The purpose of research is to obtain enough data to ask a question, answer a question, or accept/reject a hypothesis. It sounds simple enough. You decide on a question to research, select a test group, design a questionnaire, pass it out, obtain the results, tabulate them, and list the findings on paper. That's all there is to it, right? WRONG! How do you know your questionnaire is reliable (i.e., will the question be understood by those answering the questionnaire)? How do you know the questions you asked measure what you think they do? Are you qualified to do the statistical analysis? Have you done all necessary back-up work to make sure no problems will develop in the testing procedure? Laboratory experiments are subject to the same weaknesses. This chapter gives guidelines to insure you don't run into problems that will invalidate your research.

The first guideline is to get and read *The Modern Researcher*, by Jacques Barzun and Henry F. Graff (New York: Harcourt, Brace and World, 1970). This manual on "all aspects of research and writing" will prove to be an invaluable aid, covering everything from the basic principles of research to writing what you mean to say.

## What Is the Question?

Selection of a research topic needs to be approached with an eye to what is possible to complete in the amount of time you have and with the resources available to you. Rewriting the history of the Roman Empire, or even the reign of Claudius, is a bit much to take on at the graduate level. Foreign-local comparison studies would not be recommended, either. Try to set the parameters for your project such that it has a beginning and an end, and it is possible for you to do a thorough job and complete the study. You do not need to begin your life's work in graduate school — you want to get out someday. Remember that this is still a learning experience, and give yourself room to make mistakes and correct them.

Asking the question, or setting up the hypothesis, is one of the first steps in the research process. Your committee should help with both selecting a topic and framing the research design. A research proposal will be required for study at the doctoral level. If your university requires such a document for a master's project, it will be to your benefit. (Even if it isn't required, it would be helpful to you to do it.)

Don't hesitate to ask for help when you need it. It is easy to say, "Find the effects of X on Y," but it's not too easy to list a nuts-and-bolts method for finding out. You will need knowledgeable assistance to set up your research design properly. If your faculty members don't have the time or the statistical background to help you in detail, hire someone who does!

To draw up a workable research plan, you must at least know enough about the research tools to be able to ask reasonable questions. If your study is to be statistical, take a basic course in statistics. If your study will use computer analysis, take a computer course that stresses data analysis. If you're doing a sociological or psychological research study, read previous studies and observe other students conduct their research. Library studies require a knowledge of how the library works as well as being familiar with the written works in your area of interest. People perform studies all the time, not only to get information to answer questions, but also to shed more light on the information-gathering process. Review previous research in your field *before* you design your model, to determine how well the previous research plan worked.

## Obtaining Your Data

Once you have a firm idea of the question you want to answer, and if you know something about your method, the next step is to determine what information you need to get the answer. Knowing *how* the data are to be analyzed will help you determine what needs to be asked and what needs to be screened out. It will show you which questions are too broad for proper analysis. For example, a study of the buying habits of single women needs to have questions answered such as: Buying what? Does "single" mean never married, divorced, separated, widowed? With children or without? What age group? Are weight, education and religion important to the study? What about working status? These qualifying questions need to be answered before you draw up your experimental model. Otherwise, you may wind up with data that give you the characteristics of women who take the time to answer questionnaires. If you are conducting a marketing study on the potential of women consumers to buy personal computers, or the financial priorities of divorced homemakers with children, your questionnaire and analytical model must specify for these factors and filter out all the rest.

Be sure your topic is narrowed down so your analysis won't take 500 pages. Then set up a theoretical model, carry out your experimental design, and see what you get. Does it answer all your questions? Are there holes? Do you have information you don't need?

## Research Methods

"Research" can take place in many locations — in the laboratory, through questionnaires, in the library. Some research is conducted by the "scientific method," and some by library study. Most projects require a combination, for almost all projects involve some time in the library.

Libraries are where the knowledge is collected and stored and, once you have learned how to use the coding and filing system, all this information will be available to you to interpret and analyze. Most university libraries either have courses in using the library or offer an orientation session. You may need special permission to get into restricted areas, document or microfilm rooms, or historical archives. You also need to allot enough time for your library work. Hours can be guaranteed to be half as long when you are tracking down a piece of information or you're in the middle of a train of thought and need to get it down on paper before it disappears.

A caution to remember if your research topic is historical, philosophical, deals with the theoretical aspects of an applied science or performing art, or contains a literature review — in short, requires library work. The breadth of information at your disposal can lure you into broadening your topic beyond its original scope, or including information not part of the tightly-defined topic. Lacking the constraints of an experimental outline, a library study can most effectively be accomplished by using an outline method with topic sentences. You then have a ready visual reference for what is and what is not directly relevant to your subject. It requires a tremendous amount of will power to *not* use all the information you can get your hands on. There will be other projects and other papers — don't try to fit everything into one research project.

Writing an historical analysis is in some ways more difficult than writing the results of a statistical study, in that your message must be conveyed by the words you use, and there may be no numbers to fall back on for clarification. Even more attention must be paid to clarity of word usage and grammar. (Refer to Chapter 6, "Writing, Editing and Proofreading," and to the reference books listed there.)

If you are using a questionnaire, you must be certain it is designed so that your test group(s) can understand it. You can either solicit feedback from others in the field (professors, other graduate students, people connected with the group to be tested) or run a pilot study to see if you get results that make sense. (The drawback to the latter is it takes more time than most students are willing to spend.)

Bret did not have time to check out his questionnaire thoroughly before presenting it to his test groups. When he began his analysis, he found the answers were ambiguous and conflicting. Bret decided his problem was lack of understanding of how to do the statistical analysis, so he rushed to the computer center for help. The computer center staff could not assist him, and referred him to a statistician. The statistician informed Bret his questionnaire had been so poorly designed that reliable results were not obtainable. He had tried to cover too much territory, and the wording of the questions left doubt as to what was being asked. The conflicting responses were a direct result of the questionnaire design. The statistician suggested Bret discard his results and draw up a new questionnaire, getting expert advice on the design so that it was concise. Since Bret did not have time to do that, he analyzed the results, pointing out the conflicting responses. He then did an in-depth charting of the things that were wrong with his initial design. [Seeking out the necessary expertise in the beginning would have saved Bret's original project.]

In experimental studies (like recording progress of laboratory animals), you must clearly think through all stages of your research at the outset. If you slip up, there is seldom a chance to re-do the experiment.

Alexandra, a biology student, took great care to set up her field research, which involved observing the feeding pattern of individual seagulls on the mud flats during particular weather conditions. She and her team had a finely-timed schedule. They worked out the research method, watched the weather, and spent several months trapping and banding seagulls. When the time arrived for the weather/feeding studies, they arrived at the observation site only to discover they had made one small error. They had banded their seagulls on the wrong leg. When the wind shifted, the seagulls turned to face the wind, placing the tagged leg away from the experimenters' observation point so it was unreadable. The work wasn't totally wasted, but Alexandra wasn't able to realize the major objective of all the preparation work and months of planning. [More communication with faculty members experienced in field tagging would have prevented this problem.]

Honesty in experimental conduct and evaluation must also be a factor. Throwing out data that don't conform to your hypothesis does a disservice to you and to the whole research community. Twisting good data so they more closely support your hypothesis isn't ethical either.

Leo was repeating a study on the effect various stimuli and rewards had on the speed with which experimental laboratory rats ran a familiar maze. The results were comfortably within the pattern set by previous tests *except* one rat which, after running the maze successfully several times, refused to run it again. The rat instead climbed the side of the wire enclosure and hung there, observing Leo. After a week of this behavior the rat disappeared. Leo wrote up the research study with one less rat in the sample. His professor found out about the unusual rat, and Leo had to start from scratch on a new research project. [Leo was fortunate to have been allowed to remain in the program.]

## Supplemental Resources

*Courses.* Graduate students are required to take specific courses in their major to fulfill degree requirements. However, they are usually required to take only a limited number of courses in related areas which will help them in their design and analysis. If you are doing a study involving extensive data collection, take courses in statistics and computer-facilitated data analysis. The more courses you take, the greater your level of competence in designing the study and analyzing the data. Also, a course in how to do research will prove beneficial in sharpening your skills. You aren't trying to become an expert; you're trying to learn the jargon (language) and the methodology so you can know when a question needs to be asked, ask it, and identify the right answer. Don't consider such courses a waste of energy—they could save you a lot of time, money and trouble in the long run, in addition to contributing to the quality of a research project.

*Hire a statistical consultant.* Getting help when designing your experimental model will result in obtaining the data you want, and can save you trouble later. Talk it over with your committee members. If your research is incorrectly set up, you can get:
1. inaccurate or insufficient data,
2. too much data to analyze accurately,
3. data that can't be measured statistically, or
4. data that do not measure what you intended to study.
Obviously, any of the above will be frustrating and cause time problems if you must reorganize and collect new data. If you are working with people or animals, you may not have a second chance.

You could hire a consultant or a graduate student in applied mathematics, statistics or computer science to help set up your model and assist you with your statistical analysis. If your university does not have such applied programs, you could seek the help of a professor in a related area (like psychology). Remember, though, professors have a limited amount of time to assist you. If you need *extensive* assistance, hiring a consultant would be more appropriate. Balance the cost against the potential for lost time and/or unuseable data.

More than one graduate student has shown up at a typist's house with a box full of tally sheets or computer printouts and asked: "What do I do with this stuff now?" However, your typist is not the appropriate person to answer such a question—it should be asked of a qualified statistical analyst.

Nicole spent six months setting up her research and collecting data. By the time she got all the summaries together, she had a suitcase full of computer printouts—but she didn't know how to analyze it. Her typist had been recommended as someone who did a beautiful job on tables, so she thought the typist could do the analysis. Nicole arrived at the typist's door with all chapters approved except her analysis of data. She requested the typist put the data in table format, and then write the analysis. The typist explained the computer output was uninterpretable by her, and that Nicole would have to do a rough draft of the tables, adding titles and cutting and pasting the computer printouts into the format desired. She suggested that Nicole work with her committee members on the table formation, then hire a statistics graduate student to help with the data analysis. Nicole followed these suggestions and returned a month later for final typing. She admitted she had been overwhelmed by the size of the output and hadn't known where to turn for help in analyzing the data. Nicole was grateful the typist had insisted that she get the job done right, because now she and her committee members were all satisfied with the results.

Similarly, you are the only person who can be guaranteed to separate all your bibliographic entries into primary and secondary sources.

*Advisors.* Your committee is responsible for the content and factual accuracy of your research. If you are doing statistical analysis (especially if you don't have the necessary expertise), you should actively consult your advisors every step of the way. Once you have selected a general topic and have formulated a set of hypotheses, speak with them. They can assist you in areas such as: Is the topic too broad? Too narrow? Will there be enough available information? Will you have access to the intended study group? After formulating a tentative research design, again consult your advisors. They should be able to point out loopholes, blind spots, ambiguities, etc. Actively seek their assistance in the design of any questionnaire or other research tools, both for structure and validity. When analyzing your data, they will prove invaluable if they have the necessary expertise; if not, seek professional help elsewhere. In any case, your advisors have a wealth of experience and training that can be tapped. Be sure to allow enough time for consultation — your advisors can't always drop everything when you need them.

The guidance of your graduate committee is critical at all points. For example, your data may reveal the importance of a detail previously thought insignificant. They might reveal a new, more effective procedure. They might not support your hypotheses.

Consult with your advisors on how to analyze and discuss the results so they are useful to the research community. Careful wording of the text is important. If you are incorporating tables and figures, you will also need to coordinate data presentation with text. Your advisors' advice will prove invaluable in all this.

Finally, you need the signatures of all your advisors. If you don't seek their input throughout the formation and collection process, you may end up doing a lot of revising at the last stages. Better to tap their knowledge and experience, and be aware of their expectations, rather than find surprises at the end of the project. (See Chapter 9, "Revisions," for more details.)

*The Library.* Use the best library facilities available to you. This could be your university library, the public library in your city, or a larger university library thirty miles away. A university library can be relied on to have some kind of orientation, either a guided tour at intervals throughout the school term, taped tours or videotapes. University and municipal libraries are usually part of a system, and may be able to offer computerized literature searches or inter-library loans. These are time-consuming and can get to be expensive, however, so it is best to focus your search in the best facility for you, and use the system searches for specific items not available through any other method. If you are having difficulty finding your way through the library on your own, you many want to make an appointment with the reference librarian. The reference staff can point you in the right direction to find the items needed for your literature search.

## Negative Results

Did you get the results you anticipated? If so, fine; you know how to handle the write-up. If not, what can you determine from the results? Many students feel they have failed if their results did not prove statistically significant. But that does not indicate failure; they simply have learned their hypothesis was not supported. Some studies that produce negative results show specific areas where there are positive answers, or they show paths for future research to follow.

If your results are not what you originally anticipated, don't get depressed—careful analysis of your data may prove valuable in ways you had not imagined.

Sometimes students get positive results that are not statistically significant at the level they are testing. Again, this is not failure — it shows inclination in the expected direction, and future research (maybe done with a slightly different bent) could produce the results expected.

The prospect of writing a "negative" thesis has slowed down many students. But look at the positive side of it. Here is a hypothesis or procedure that has now been tested and can be discarded. This knowledge will save time and effort in future research. Fall back on the old maxim that no knowledge is useless. Add a "recommendations for future research" section to your paper, with suggestions for using the data you did get and for avoiding the problems you encountered.

## Presenting the Results

How you display the material can determine how effective it is, both for you to use and for your readers to interpret. (See Chapter 10, "Graphics.") Photographs and line drawings are effective. For some data, a tabular display is appropriate. If your data are extremely complicated, scattergrams, bar graphs or other graphic methods may be appropriate. A tabular or graphic display of the data should be free-standing, such that the reader doesn't have to go to the text to understand it. It should be possible to read the text without having to check the graphs. They should be used to present a more detailed breakdown of information if the reader wants it. Label tables and caption figures clearly enough that they can be understood out of context if necessary.

Equally important, you don't have to use all your data. You may have collected enough data for two studies, but your thesis is focused on one aspect of it. So, write your thesis, sticking to its topic. Once you have completed the thesis, analyze the excess data for an expanded study or for publication in a journal. Similarly, your thesis will not be enhanced by 32 pages of computer printouts or tally sheets, which no one is going to look at or understand. The thesis is the summary and compilation of the data — not a place to reproduce all of it.

However, if you do omit material in the final product, be sure you don't omit something that was necessary. More than one paper has been written giving the intricate details of a statistical study, leaving out the simple fact of how many samples were taken out of a total population of what size. How valid are electron micrograph photos without the magnification? Or a study on the growth of any organism that doesn't mention the temperature? Or a survey on religious beliefs which doesn't mention that all the persons interviewed had just come out of a church service? (Or a Sunday football game?)

After you have written up the results of your research, *look at it again*. What was your original question? Have you answered it, or have you approached another question? Have you raised more questions than you answered? Have you thoroughly confused the reader?

Remember that your research must be documented in such a way that someone else can replicate your study. This duplication is done all the time and serves (1) to corroborate your work, and (2) to seek further information from your work. If you were not looking for X, but for Y and Z, another person could duplicate your research method and concentrate on X under those same circumstances. If you studied junior high students, someone could duplicate your study at the high school level. If you studied private school students, someone may wish to duplicate the study using public school children. It is more of an honor to have your thesis followed up and quoted as research worthy of more study than to simply have it stored away on a shelf.

## *Conclusion*

Great care must be taken in setting up your research model not to get lost — to lose sight of the forest for the trees.

The design of your experiment, collection of data and analysis of results must be conducted with considerable forethought and planning. The object is to produce quality work with reliable results that can be replicated in future studies. Doing the job right will be rewarding to you. In fact, it may serve as the beginning of continued graduate work at the Ph.D. level or provide the base for your first published article. Treat it carefully!

## *Dos and Don'ts*

Do:

Involve your committee in all aspects of design, collection, and analysis of data.

Confer with your committee to build a working bibliography.

Take appropriate courses to help you do the research and analyze the data.

Hire necessary expertise in designing and analyzing the data.

After you have analyzed your data, check it again — did you answer the question you proposed, or ask new questions?

Set up and document your research in such a way that it can be replicated by someone else.

Don't:

Expect a statistics or computer science graduate student to make sense of your results unless the design and collection of data were formulated properly.

Manipulate data to obtain results you wanted.

Get depressed if your results are not what you anticipated.

Expect your typist to do the data analysis for you, or the structuring of your tables from computer printouts — that's *your* job.

Include unnecessary data in your thesis — it can be published separately in a journal article.

Think no one will ever look at your research, so it doesn't have to be documented correctly — your research could be the basis for someone else's study in the future.

Think that if your design is faulty you can easily retrace your steps and redo the work.

Make your topic too broad to cover adequately within your time and resource limits.

## Chapter 6
# Writing, Editing and Proofreading

After completing major graduate courses (the familiar) comes the writing of the thesis (the unfamiliar). It isn't as unfamiliar as it seems when you look at it closely, and with proper committee guidance it doesn't have to be a traumatic experience — most professors require a preliminary outline as part of the thesis proposal. However, many students do run into problems with writing and editing. This chapter will deal with the major questions that come up and aren't covered by the style manual, or are covered but need to be applied to thesis-level academic writing. "Writing" actually encompasses three areas — writing, editing and proofreading. Each is discussed in depth. The object is to make the burden of writing your thesis a little lighter, and to help you end up with a finished product that says what you want it to, and that you can be proud to put your name on.

Two references will provide valuable assistance:

William Strunk, Jr. and E.B. White, *The Elements of Style* (New York: Macmillan, 1979). A slim (78 pages) volume, worth more than its $3 cost, it contains a crash course in basic writing.

Jacques Barzun and Henry F. Graff, *The Modern Researcher* (New York: Harcourt, Brace and World, 1977). This more comprehensive volume (hardback, $13) has an excellent chapter on "Footnotes and Bibliography," as well as more in-depth treatment of research techniques and writing.

## Writing

Writing doesn't really come first. Thinking and planning do. Planning in turn breaks the writing process down into several component parts: the title, chapters, headings and subheadings, and getting the words onto paper.

## Title

This may be the hardest part of your thesis to write — it forces you to put down in very few words what it's all about. Remember that your title is a title, not an abstract. Too long, and it tries to convey too much information and may wind up lessening its impact and confusing the reader. Too short, and it doesn't convey enough information. It needs to be a capsule statement of your main topic, including the main issues or variables you have investigated.

When writing your title, keep in mind any limitations imposed by the graduate school — some have length limits based on the number of letters and spaces that can be imprinted on the book's spine. After your title is written, pretend you're coding key words for *Dissertation Abstracts*. How would you code this title? Is that what your study is about?

Surprising though it is to some people, it's a good idea to write the title *first*. Then you have a constant reminder throughout the rest of your paper — does this paragraph contribute to the topic stated in the title? Writing the manuscript first and then trying to figure out what it was about is backwards and more difficult.

## Chapters

What goes into a thesis and where does it go? Here's a brief summary of the chapters in a thesis based on a research topic:

1. *Introduction.* What the study is about. What the problem is, why you selected it, the theories you propose to investigate, and in general terms how you plan to go about it. All this should have been thought out before you began your project. A trip to the library will serve only to fill in the blanks or missing specifics in this section.

2. *Background or Literature Review.* A review of research conducted by others in your general field of study. It sometimes includes research methods used in other fields that you want to apply to yours. The exact references will depend on your approach and topic, but should always include a survey and brief description of the past and current research. You aren't starting off cold in your

area—other people did the groundwork needed even to raise the question you're investigating. Discuss the previous research in view of your project, pointing out what worked and what did not work in earlier studies. This chapter is practically written in the library before you begin your own work.

A note is in order on references. When you go to the library, write down all the information you need for a correct citation (according to the style manual you will be using): author or editor, title of article and journal or book, chapter number and title, publisher and city, volume and number, page numbers (including the page number of any direct quotations), and any other publication data. (Refer again to Barzun and Graff.) It can be very hard to relocate a book once it's out of your grasp. Failure to note the proper information in the first place can result in a lot of wasted hours tracking down the article again (or in having some gaps in your final product) when all you need may be the page numbers of an article or a quotation, or the place and date of publication. The object of all this information is so another person can go back to the references you have cited and read them.

3. *Methods.* A painstakingly detailed and clearly written description of your research method. This chapter is easy to write. Simply, what did you do? If someone else were to duplicate your work, what information would they need? What size pipettes were used? How much of what kind of growth medium? How many students? What age, sex, race, and so forth? Every detail is important—someone else might want to use your study as a control, but change one detail and measure the effects. Included in this information should be your reasons for doing anything in a particular way—if you selected an item or procedure on purpose instead of by arbitrary decision. Likewise, if you changed part of the procedure or materials during your study, say so and explain why. All these minor details are important contributions to the knowledge being collected by you and other researchers in your field of study.

4. *Results or Analysis of the Data.* The previous chapter described how your data were collected. This chapter describes what you did with the information. This is the chapter that will have the most tables and figures, to show in both graphic and narrative form the information you collected. All of your raw data do not need to be presented here, only that which pertains to your study. If you have additional data, you might say so (so someone else could contact you if they need it) or include it as an appen-

dix. However, raw data are almost incomprehensible to anyone else. This chapter is where you present your data, but not your conclusions. In some theses "Discussion of Results" is a subsection of the Results chapter, and the Findings chapter contains the conclusions. It depends on the field of study.

5. *Findings or Conclusions.* This chapter is frequently the shortest chapter in a thesis. It returns to the hypotheses outlined in the introduction and reviews each in light of the data presented. You should be able to say that each was accepted or not, based on your interpretation of the data. Some students have problems with the "not" — writing a negative thesis. Even though we all would like to write the cornerstone work on which all future research is based, there aren't very many of those. Your contributions confirming what does not work are just as important as someone else's confirmation of what does work. You have saved yourself or some other researcher a lot of time and effort chasing down the wrong path of a maze. Or, you have shown that this method does not work with these materials, under these circumstances, at this time. Every contribution, every datum, is valuable. The conclusions chapter of many theses contains a "suggestions for further research" section that lists not only directions for future research built upon the present study, but also pitfalls to avoid in similar work.

6. *References or Bibliography.* References are those works you have referred to or cited in your paper. They will have been noted in the text by "Smith (1981)" or as a footnote and full citation, depending on the format you are using. While "references" list only those works referred to in your paper, a "bibliography" lists those works, as well as background literature you referred to and found useful, although not specifically cited in your paper. Some bibliographies are annotated, with a brief explanation of the key points of the article. Each style manual has very specific directions for the way bibliographic entries are to be cited. It's critical to check this before your trip to the library. Also read Chapter 15, "Footnotes and Bibliography," in Barzun and Graff.

7. *Appendices.* An appendix is a repository for work you want to include in your thesis, but which isn't appropriate in the main body. Common inclusions are: digressions that are important as background to your work, but their inclusion in the main body world break the flow of thought and distract the reader; tables needed to obtain a number needed to plug into an equation in the text; your computer printouts; a copy of the questionnaire, survey,

or test administered to a group; lesson plans. In short, the parts of your research tools needed to illustrate your methods, or the bulk data from which your conclusions are drawn, belong in an appendix.

We've just outlined a thesis. All the pieces and parts are there, and it's in reasonable order. Now that you know what should go in and where it should go, let's take a look at putting it there.

## Headings and Subheadings

The general framework of your thesis is built around the broad categories (chapters) outlined above. Within each chapter will be a number of sub-topics. As an example, look at the Table of Contents of this book. The text is in five main parts. Part I contains only one chapter, Part II has three chapters, Part III has six chapters (of which this chapter is one), and so forth. Within this chapter are three main sections: Writing, Editing, and Proofreading. Within the Writing section are the subsections Title, Chapters, Headings and Subheadings, Getting the Words on Paper, and How Long Should It Be?

This is basic outline structure. It can help organize your material, note information for emphasis, clarify specific thoughts. Using a working outline as a tool to help write your paper provides a structure, and shows were to put pieces of information. In its final form, it's the table of contents to your paper.

Each style manual has its own rules for levels of headings, but in general subheadings are visual cues to show the importance of the information in each section relative to the information in the rest of the chapter. Not every paper uses all levels of subheadings, but it is important not to use them out of order.

## Getting the Words on Paper

If your paper is structured at the outset—in your head or in outline form—the hardest part of the work is done. You may feel comfortable organizing the whole document mentally before pen is ever put to paper. If your head is like a sieve, as heads tend to become when the stress mounts in the later stages of graduate school, you may prefer to use index cards or a working outline. Make it a multi-level outline. Then flesh it out by writing a few sentences. Next, change the sentences into paragraphs. That way, you will be assured of keeping each topic and subtopic concise, and you will have a visual sense of what has been done and what is left to do.

Another way to tackle the content aspect of your thesis is to shut yourself away and dump out everything you know onto paper. Let it get cold, then reread it, axe parts of it with bloodthirsty abandon, and cut and paste what's left into a reasonable document. For those who write best this way, it is very efficient. It also makes a satisfying mess on the floor.

For some people it is easier to systematically build a project, and for others it's easier to throw everything together and then organize it. It depends on how you work best. Take a minute to review how you wrote your previous papers, remembering how successful you were with the method you used and how well you survived the writing process. Then decide which method (or combination) is best for you to undertake when writing your thesis or dissertation.

This encouragement to get your words down on paper must be accompanied by a caution not to use too many of them. If your tendency is to write as you would talk, the end result is that the document turns out to be three times as long as it needs to be. Use only as many words as are necessary to clearly say what you mean.

Another possible problem area is the use of jargon. When writing for a specialized technical journal, you can determine the right amount of jargon to use by reading other articles in that journal. When writing a thesis or dissertation, or for a journal with more general readership, jargon must be used sparingly. Consider that your work will be read and, hopefully, understood by people doing library research for a variety of purposes. One guideline is to see how well you understand it yourself. It is said that Ernest Hemmingway tested every word he wrote by trying the sentence without the word. Can your writing survive without jargon? Does it rely too heavily on it? Can you define a jargon word without using another jargon word? It should be possible to write what you intend in plain, simple English. If you choose to use some jargon, then define it in plain, simple English. This can be done in the text after the first use of the word, as is done for abbreviations, or you can include a glossary.

Another aspect of thesis or dissertation writing that sets it apart from the term papers you have written or the novel you plan, is that it is your academic masterwork. It should by no means be dry and lifeless, but it's not the place for statements of unsubstantiated opinion or cute turns of phrase. It must be a solid research or creative effort (depending on your field of study) that conveys a feeling of competence by the way it is written. But don't be afraid of your own medium. It is possible to fall into the trap of feeling you must "sound" scholarly, and that leads to tripping over the words and getting lost in them. Every paragraph has a thought to communicate. It's best to do it in as straightforward a manner as possible: use active, not passive, verbs; use terms the reader can picture; vary the length of sentences — some short, some long. Avoid unneeded words. And stay away from "obviously, inasmuch as, therefore, however, thus, nevertheless!" Again, refer to the guidelines in Strunk and White.

The preceding paragraphs may sound contradictory: Write! — but not too much; be professional — but don't use jargon or sound stuffy. The real criterion is that it must meet your committee's standards, and yours. It is your thesis. It must communicate what you intended to say in a manner that is understandable by your readers. In the long run, only you will be responsible for the quality of the research effort and the written product.

## How Long Should It Be?

This simple question has been the cause of great concern among students. Is my thesis too short? Do you think I've said enough? How long is the average thesis? My friend's thesis was half the size of mine, have I added more information than necessary? Such uneasiness is normal and expected, and the answer to the question is unsatisfying: Your thesis should be as long as it needs to be to cover your topic — no longer and no shorter.

Include everything that is necessary to your topic, and analyze it completely. When you have done that, you are finished. The size of the thesis will largely depend on your topic. For example, heavily scientific areas usually produce very short theses. Theses in education are generally long, because they include lengthy appendices of tables or lesson plans. An original composition for an English degree may be a series of short stories, with a total of only 30 text pages. A counseling experiment could take 50 pages just for the data analysis chapter if a series of hypotheses was studied. If a great deal of research has been done in your field, your literature review chapter may comprise the bulk of your thesis. (One student moaned, "I should *never* have picked a topic that 200 people have worked on before me!") The "average" thesis is 75 to 150 pages; dissertations are generally longer, averaging 150 to 250 pages. These are only averages, with the range of sizes being quite broad:

Karma's graduate project was to derive an equation to approximate a solution to an "unsolvable" mathematics problem. She accomplished this task, and produced a thesis that had more obligatory format pages (approval, title, acknowledgements, contents, references) than it did text pages. The entire thesis was less than 20 pages long.

Guenevere wrote a 350-page dissertation analyzing one chapter of one book of the *Bible*. [Students studying theology can produce lengthy theses/dissertations because of extensive research and discussion of other sources, in addition to quotations from the *Bible*.]

Lance wrote a 150-page thesis that was extremely wordy. At the beginning of each chapter he extensively reviewed the work in all previous chapters. By the time he reached chapter 6, he had 25 pages of review covering chapters 1 through 5. Lance commented to the typist that he realized there was a lot of repetition in his work, but he felt it needed to be 150 pages long to present his material. [A 30% cut would have been realistic, allowing for short review of previous work and cutting out unnecessary repetition.]

## Editing

Everyone's concept of editing seems to be different and many students don't think they need it. One definition offered by *The Random House Dictionary of the English Language*, unabridged edition (New York: Random House, 1969), is "to revise or correct, as a manuscript." That's pretty open-ended. That's also why everyone's concept of editing is different. There are many levels of editing, as well as many degrees of competence. There are also the questions of who is to do it and how much is necessary.

Assuming you are not going to give your first draft manuscript to your committee for review (or second, or maybe even third), what you do to it between drafts is editing. If not the whole manuscript, certainly some chapters or sections will probably undergo extensive revision. It is the massaging and transforming of what you wrote the first time into what you want to say, and would be willing to show in public with your name on it.

## Levels of Editing

*Level 1* is revising the draft manuscript according to the required format, such as Campbell-Ballou, Turabian, MLA, APA. Each of these formats has specific requirements governing style of footnotes, bibliography and references, citations in text, quotations, style of chapter headings, and so forth. A good thesis typist will be familiar with the style required by your department, but it would simplify your organization if you were familiar with the required format and wrote it that way to begin with.

This level of editing also encompasses such mundane things as punctuation and spelling. Use of commas and other punctuation will, to some degree, be governed by the style manual and university regulations. In some cases punctuation is discretionary, but your usage must be consistent.

Spelling is a little less neat, and how difficult it is depends on your topic. Some people naturally know how to spell well, and others just have to try harder. If your spelling is terrible, it may be possible for your typist to correct it during typing, determining what the word should be from the context. But if your topic is technical, or uses jargon words and scientific terms which don't occur in everyday language, you cannot rely on your typist's spelling ability to catch errors. At the same time, it is critically important to have everything in your paper spelled correctly—it's a reflection on your general competence and attention to detail. One solution to the spelling problem is to have an impartial third party (who knows your topic *and* can spell) read your paper after it is typed. Another, more versatile suggestion is to look up each difficult word once, and make a list of correctly spelled words for your typist to refer to—then you don't have to worry about it.

Unfortunately it is not a good practice to rely on committee members to correct your punctuation and spelling. Some can spell and some can't, and if you can't spell it's hard to tell the difference. When approving a rough draft, faculty committee members tend to be more concerned with the content and factual accuracy of the paper, saving the chore of correcting spelling, grammar, and punctuation for someone else, or assuming you'll clean it up for the final draft. But your committee members will pick out errors and inconsistencies after the final typing. Regardless of who does (or does not do) this level of editing, you are still responsible for the final outcome!

Another area of difficulty with committee members is that they may have strong opinions on style and format which are in conflict with your university requirements. This can be handled by getting one or the other to bend. Sometimes the university isn't concerned about specific format, so long as the document is consistent within itself; other universities will not accept a thesis that does not conform to all university standards. If the latter is the case, you must inform your committee members that the work will be rejected if the regulations are not adhered to. The professors will have to bend. If this question arises, it can't be avoided, but must be dealt with quickly and directly.

*Level 2* is where the grammer comes in. Grammar and sentence structure require a good working knowledge of the English language. Common problems in this area include consistency of tense, agreement of subject and verb, use of modifiers, parallel sentence structure, and excess verbiage. Consistency of tense gets to be a bit tricky, especially in research papers. The portion of the work that refers to the research project itself must be written in the past tense. Papers referenced in the text are also referred to in the past tense ("The results showed...."). The conclusions which say that further work must be done can properly be in present and future tense. Keeping the tenses straight, especially when your research notes are probably written in present tense, may be something you need to pay separate attention to after the first draft is written.

Agreement of subject and verb is another major area of downfall for writers. "Data" is plural, but one rarely sees the singular word "datum" in use. (The traditional example is "scissors," which refers to a pair of blades, even though there's only one instrument in your hand.) The verb in a listed series of singular items will be plural ("a, b, c, and d *are* in agreement"). These rules will also be listed in your style manual.

Sentence structure and placement of modifiers must be carefully monitored, so your meaning is not misunderstood. Misplaced modifiers offer bright spots of hilarity in research papers. Some favorite examples are:

The author spotted the pelicans at 30 yards, and his assistant at 50 yards. [Was the assistant 50 yards away, or did the assistant spot the pelicans 50 yards away?]

The area consists of many older homes that preceded local zoning regulations which have deep and irregularly shaped lots. [The regulations have deep and irregularly shaped lots?]

Twelve acres are located within the 251-acre special studies zone, of which 4.5 acres are vacant. [Are the 4.5 acres within the 12 acres or within the 251-acre special studies zone?]

Practice takeoffs/landings and instrument approaches are conducted when individuals are normally awake. [We should hope so!]

*Level 3* is the substantive level. This is what you do after the first draft has come back with notations all over it: "expand this," "delete," "what are you trying to say here?" "give examples," "rewrite." After you have written all your chapters (most likely at different times and out of order), you will find some duplication among them. Culling this out and putting information in its proper place, adding topics, expanding some and cutting down others, is substantive editing. It means dealing with the content and structure of the document as a whole, rather than on a paragraph and sentence level. This is the area where your committee will be heavily involved. At this level you must state your hypotheses and see if your research has proved them. The final test is whether the paper is actually about what the title promised it would be.

## Ethics

The question of ethics must be approached when talking about editing. If your writing, spelling and grammar are poor, and your committee members are not willing to undertake this for you, the possibility of hiring an editor or even a ghost writer may occur to you. Talk it over with your committee. Remember, this document must be a reflection of *your* skills and ability. The question is whether it must be a reflection of your writing and spelling skills as well. As a completed and bound document, it is also a reflection of the standards of your university. Some people are so frozen or burned out when it comes to the final stages of thesis preparation that they are literally unable to formulate another way to say something. Others are trying to skate through and collect the degree without spilling the blood that is required. For some fields, technical competence is stressed but writing skill is not.

A good editor can straighten out your grammar, correct your spelling and punctuation, and *help* make the revisions your committee has required, while still maintaining the integrity of your work. It is a matter of assuming you have the knowledge, but need help expressing it.

Bernie had good command of spoken language but very little confidence in his writing ability. His committee members didn't want to take the time to work with him, so they suggested he find an editor who would. Working with Bernie was often a matter of saying, "What did you mean to say here?" and then copying down his verbal response. He was afraid of the written medium.

Ghost writing is a totally different matter. Here you are taking someone else's work and putting your name to it, and collecting the academic rewards and recognition. It is not ethical, it will probably catch up with you in the long run, and if you were considering it you probably wouldn't have bought this book.

## Finding an Editor

If you decide to hire an editor, be sure it is with your committee's approval. In some cases, the recommendation to find an editor comes from the committee members!

Andres was a foreign student whose thesis was well organized, but whose word usage patterns identified him as a non-native speaker of English. He also occasionally used the wrong verb tense or misused a word. His typist/editor read the draft before typing it and modified his writing to standard English. The additional cost was not great, and prevented the language problem from detracting from the quality of the work.

Find an editor in much the same way as you found your typist. You might even begin by getting a recommendation from your typist. Check with the graduate office, your department, your committee members. As an alternative, your university's English or journalism department may offer courses in editing, and have advanced students who are competent to work with you. An editor must be well founded in English grammar and word usage, and have impeccable spelling skills. Experience in academic editing, preferably in your field, is also a requirement.

Charges for editing are almost invariably by the hour, since how long it takes to work through a paper depends entirely on the amount of work it needs. If your paper is well organized but you need help with the spelling and grammar, it should not take very long (about six to ten pages per hour). If your paper requires substantial revision and some writing of transitions or working in committee revisions, two to four pages per hour may be more accurate. You may want to ask the editor to work long enough to get a feel for your paper, and then call you with an estimate. The difference in whether the final document has been edited or not is like the difference between typing on a correcting electric or on a portable. A well-edited document will say what you meant to, regardless of what you actually put down on paper in your draft. But remember, *you* are responsible for the outcome — work closely with your editor so that the content remains yours.

Ira was nearing deadlines on all fronts. His seven-year limit to remain in graduate school was approaching, and his employer had given him notice that the thesis must be approved by the deadline he had agreed upon or he would lose his job. Ira had submitted several drafts of his thesis, and all had been returned with requests for revision. Unfortunately, the notations for revision were vague and seemed to be contradictory. Ira was immobilized and could not think of more new ways to say the same thing, so took all the drafts and comments to an editor. The editor was able to sort out the weaknesses in the document and determine what the questions of the reviewers were. She made a list of all the questions she and the reviewers had noted, interviewed Ira at length, and then incorporated his answers into the document. The next draft of the thesis was approved, and Ira received his degree and kept his job.

## Proofreading

Proofreading is much more than reading a typed draft for mistakes. It is a quality control step which must be taken several times, each time with a specific purpose. For example, before you deliver each draft to your typist, read it for content. Do all your cut-and-pastings make sense, or was something important left on the floor while another paragraph was repeated? Can you easily follow all your own notations and inserts? After the typed draft has been returned to you, read it again. Did the typist understand all your notes? Are there any typographical errors?

Careful proofreading of the draft would have spotted this beautiful example of a cut-and-paste accident:

The visual quality of the main road would benefit from the proximity to the green spine and would be far superior to the typical monotonous layout of houses on a double-loaded street after street with no contact to any significant natural features with a typical experience of rows and rows of homes along a double-loaded street corridor.

This sentence was easy to spot as having something wrong with it. Other errors are more difficult—especially spelling and word hyphenation. Minor spelling errors are often missed in proofing because the reader—particularly if the material is familiar—will see what is supposed to be there rather than what really is. Likewise, many people are not all that sure about hyphenation. Even putting your work on a word processor does not completely solve these problems.

Spelling-check software only recognizes misspelled words, not homonyms or correctly spelled words used out of context. For example, transposing letters, or adding or omitting a letter or two, makes the following context-altering changes the computer will *not* flag:

| | | |
|---|---|---|
| nuclear | to | unclear |
| united | to | untied |
| interstate | to | intestate |
| plaque | to | plague |
| ripple | to | tipple |
| six | to | sex |

Some of these may also result when the typist mistakes an unfamiliar word in your draft for a typo (or can't read your writing), and "corrects" it to an incorrect word.

Hyphenation features in word processing programs break words according to the most common rules of grammatical usage. But the English language is known for its exceptions, and "correct" hyphenations are not always acceptable. For example, Wednesday is hyphenated Wednes-day, not Wed-nesday. It's chil-dren, not child-ren. Suffixes and prefixes are trouble spots because separating one or two letters at the beginning or end of a word [re-type, random-ly, a-bility] is not acceptable in manuscript typing. Words with double consonants and suffixes are often mishyphenated [fal-ling instead of fall-ing]. Some university regulations also specifically prohibit separating a suffix or prefix from the root word [con-, sub-, or -tion, -ing]. Some universities or departments prefer the more conservative practice of hyphenating a word after the stressed syllable, even though other divisions are accurate [frontiers-man instead of fron-tiersman].

Proofreading your draft twelve times may not sound like a lot of fun, and you may not have the time to do it, but the accuracy of proofreading increases markedly when the draft is read several times, checking specific things with each reading. Consider getting someone else who is not deeply involved in your thesis to read and help finalize it — searching for inconsistencies. Working from that person's list would take less of your time and still assure a high accuracy level. Here's a list of things to look for *before* the draft is taken for final typing.

1. Check all numbers in text and tables against your original notes.

2. Check all computations for accuracy.

3. Read the text for writing style and organization.

4. Check spelling, grammar and punctuation.

5. Make sure the draft is page-numbered.

6. Are all the figures and tables accounted for, and do they have legends or titles?

7. Are your headings and subheadings in proper order?

8. Are all citations in the bibliography complete and accurate?

9. Are all footnotes accurate, and do they match the listing in the bibliography?

10. Are all inserts and deletions clearly marked?

*After* the typed draft has been returned to you, read it again:

1. Are there any typographical errors?

2. Are all numbers and symbols correct?

3. Is it accurately page-numbered?

4. Are the titles and page numbers in the table of contents and lists of figures and tables accurate?

5. Does the typing conform to the requirements of the university and the style manual?

6. Is anything "missing" that you have to do (like mount photographs)?

This painstaking thoroughness is the only way to achieve an error-free final product. Someone along the line (your committee, department, or the graduate office) will find the errors you have missed or skipped, and bounce the document back for corrections. The result is lost time and added expense. Careful reading before the final typing will reduce the number of errors in the final copy, and proofreading after typing will reduce the number of errors other readers find. It *is* possible to produce a "perfect" document.

## Conclusions

Many students experience difficulty with the mechanics of writing or revising their thesis, partly because they do not know how to go about it. If effort is put into thinking it through before the writing starts, the process will be greatly simplified. Special attention does need to be paid to structure, word usage, grammar and spelling, but it all contributes to a better final product. It can be difficult to write a thesis, especially if you feel uncomfortable with your writing skills, but stick with it. It will get done! The student who said, "Take care of this stack of papers — it represents three years of my life!" spoke for everyone who has been to graduate school.

After your thesis has been written, edited, typed and proofread, you may feel you deserve a separate degree in perseverance, bureaucracy, and diplomacy. You do!

## *Dos and Don'ts*

Do:

Expect to do extensive editing before final submission.
Check your style manual for specifics on writing style and format.
Keep *exact* and complete information for footnotes and bibliography (the book may be gone when you try to find it again later).
Be consistent in spelling, punctuation (following correct format).
Watch sentence structure and grammar — say what you mean.
Use subheadings for organization and clarity.
Hire a professional editor if you need one.

Carefully proofread the draft before and after each typing.

Don't:

Expect your first draft to be approved unchanged.

Rely on committee members to correct spelling and punctuation — they might do it *after* the final typing has been paid for.

Make your title too long or too short.

Worry about the size of your thesis — say what needs to be said, then stop!

Hire someone to write all or portions of your thesis — that's unethical.

Be afraid of writing — you can learn and improve your methods.

Expect "someone else" to proofread your thesis, unless you make such an arrangement.

# Chapter 7
# You and Your Typist

After selecting your committee, perhaps the single most important decision you will make pertaining to processing your thesis is selecting your typist. For every successful encounter with a typist there may be a counterbalancing horror story. There are good and bad typists, as well as good and bad students to type for; you will be responsible for selecting and being one of the good ones.

This chapter deals with such questions as: Can I type the thesis myself (or have my wife/friend do it)? How do I select a good typist? If I live far away from campus, should my typist be close to me, or close to the university? What questions do I need to ask/answer in an initial phone inquiry with a typist? What does my typist expect from me? What can I expect from my typist? How is the bill determined? If I have problems with my typist, how can they be resolved?

## Typing It Yourself

If you are a good typist, you may want to consider doing the typing yourself, rather than paying for professional services. In making this decision, first determine whether the equipment you plan to use meets university standards. (Normally an electric typewriter with carbon ribbon is required; a correction device is highly desirable since universities usually have specific requirements concerning corrections.) If your own typewriter is not adequate, rentals are available from office supply firms. Typewriter rentals are usually on a monthly basis, and require a security deposit. If you rent a typewriter, test it before you leave the store. Find out the service procedure and responsibility if a mechanical problem arises. In case of loss, theft or damage beyond regular wear in the machine, you and your personal insurance will be responsible for repair or replacement costs. And be sure you have enough typewriter ribbons, correction tapes, and the right kind of paper!

Assuming you have the skill, it is important to determine if you also have the time and patience to type your own thesis. Every professional typist has heard "I could have typed it myself" from clients whose reasons for not doing it include:

•I have too much else to do.
•I can't proofread my own typing.
•I'm getting too stressed to do a good job.
•I'm concerned about the university regulations.
•Every time I type a draft I change something.
•I don't want to look at it again until it's finished.
•I'm going to take a short vacation instead.

The next thing to do is get a copy of your university requirements and the appropriate style manual. Specific university regulations are usually available through the graduate office (see Chapter 3, "University Regulations," for a discussion). Failure to comply with these directions could result in rejection of the final product! The style manual required by your department will give the format for typing manuscripts in your field of study. In cases of conflict between the two, the university regulations always take precedence.

After reading these two sources you will be able to decide if you want to type it yourself. If you feel confident, but have a few questions, you may find it worthwhile to make an appointment with a professional thesis typist to discuss basic instructions and guidelines, and things to watch for such as discrepancies between style manual and university requirements. Paying for an hour of the typist's time could save you considerable headache! [We must note at this point that reference to typist, thesis typist, or professional typist throughout this chapter refers to a typist who *routinely* works for universities and graduate students, and is therefore familiar with school requirements and the commonly-used style manuals. Many independent typists and secretarial services are highly skilled, but are not familiar with the special requirements of academic typing.]

Simon read the style manual and noted there must be a triple space between previous text and subheadings. Not being used to the language of typing manuals, he interpreted "triple space" to mean three *double* spaces; in fact, it means three *single* spaces. Simon's thesis was rejected by the graduate office.

## Friendship Typing

Students sometimes rely on the typing skills of spouses or friends to get them through school and submission of their theses. This can work beautifully, or it can be a complete disaster, causing unnecessary stress within a marriage or friendship. Keep in mind that you are under stress while in graduate school, and it may affect your behavior more than you think it does. (See Chapter 11, "Stress," and Chapter 13, "You and Your Family and Friends.") Also consider that no service is rendered "for free." If you're going to your spouse or friend for typing, are you prepared to compensate for their time and effort? List them in your acknowledgments, buy them a good dinner, a dozen roses, or a case of wine — do something to show your gratitude.

Another aspect of friendship typing is communication. People often speak to or treat people close to them in a way they would not consider treating a stranger. In pointing out errors and corrections in typing, be careful that you do not make it sound like personal criticism.

"How could you make a dumb mistake like that?"

"It's obvious from looking at it that it's supposed to be _____ and not _____."

"You put an 'a' here instead of an 'e'."

"You didn't follow the arrows here. You should have put this here instead of down there."

This approach can cause resentment that lasts long after the thesis is submitted. Don't make the assumption that because the person you're living with or close to is doing the typing, they are always at your disposal. Don't call your friend in the middle of the night or at work to give instructions, make insertions or change things. If your spouse is trying to fix dinner or read the kids a bedtime story, wait until you can get his or her full attention before giving instructions on your thesis.

Not being able to stop working on your manuscript presents a greater hazard when it's being typed on a friendship basis. If it's being typed practically under your nose, the temptation is almost overwhelming to start making changes as soon as each page is out of the typewriter. These are hard working conditions, and have resulted in more than one half-final-typed thesis being brought to a professional typist. ("My wife was going to type it for me and it looks just fine; I don't understand why she didn't want to finish it.")

The success of friendship typing will depend entirely on your communication skills and your relationship with the typist. You will have to work this out. Here are two examples with opposite endings:

Nate was a doctoral candidate in chemistry. His wife was a good typist, so she agreed to type the dissertation. Although she had access to a typewriter with the necessary chemical symbols, she found it difficult to do the technical typing involved in chemical formulas. Nate can laugh about the stress many years later, but it is still a sore subject with his wife! [Any typist not used to doing chemical typing would have found the project difficult; but in this case it was compounded by also living with the author. At least one of the parties in this case has said the money saved was *not* worth the trauma.]

Edwin was a master's candidate in biology. His wife was a professional thesis typist, but planned to arrange for an associate to type the thesis. However, Edwin was dangerously close to his seven-year limit, and was working full time. The introduction and literature review were written, and he had finished the research project long ago, but was having trouble finishing the thesis. Working from his original outline and laboratory notes, Edwin wrote section by section, and his wife edited and typed each page as he wrote it. She delivered the chapters to his major professor and helped with the revisions. Edwin realized he would not have received the degree without his wife's active participation, and wrote a touching acknowledgment to thank her for it.

As you can see, these two cases worked out differently, perhaps because one wife was a thesis typist and the other wasn't. The husband's perception of the wife's contribution differed in each case, also. However, both wives had additional stress in the marriage because of being involved in the production of their husband's graduate work.

Students often expect to pay a friend a lower rate than they would pay a professional typist. This is between you and your friend. If this is the case, be sure this arrangement is satisfactory with your friend; be sure the friend is qualified and has the appropriate equipment; and be sure to broach the touchy subject of corrections. Unfortunately, after typing the thesis, your friend may feel the obligation is settled, and you're on your own for corrections and revisions. Likewise, if your friend's work fails to meet university standards, you may be forced to hire another typist anyway.

If your friend is a professional typist, you may find the friend-ship contribution is in squeezing your work into an already busy schedule, and not in reduced rates. If your spouse or friend is un-willing to type your thesis, accept the refusal as a sign of wisdom and not rejection.

You may find yourself in the awkward position  of having to handle the reverse situation — a friend who types and wants to type your thesis, but you don't think is qualified. Here are some ready-made reasons/excuses for not accepting the well-intentioned offer:

•The draft is such a mess, I know there will be a lot of revisions, and I don't want to put you through that.

•There will be a lot of revisions, so I want to put it on a word processor.

•I've already made arrangements with a typist who has done a lot of work for students in my department and is familiar with the subject matter.

•I appreciate your offer, but I've already made other arrangements.

Additional things to consider when thinking about typing the thesis yourself or having it done on a friendship basis:

1.  A nonprofessional typist who is unfamiliar with the style manual and your university's regulations may take longer to type it because of the format research involved.

2.  If your thesis requires any special typing skills (mathematics, chemical formulas, charts, figures, tables, graphs, symbols, foreign language) do you have the ability and equipment to produce ac-ceptable quality? (See Chapter 10, "Graphics and Special Typing Needs," for more details.)

3.  If the work is unacceptable to the university, will you have time to retype it and still make your deadline for submission?

4.  If you type it yourself, it's very important to get someone else to proofread the final copy — preferably someone who is familiar with the subject area but who has never read your manuscript.

## Summary

Is it possible to do the job yourself? Yes. However, you have to follow the regulations, and take necessary steps to see that the job is done correctly. Proper equipment, skills and guidance are needed. If you are willing to spend the time to make sure the job is done right, you can be successful. Is it *advisable?* In most cases, NO! Most students don't have the time, equipment, patience, or skills to type their own thesis/dissertation. Their time and energy is usually better spent on other facets of their graduate career, thus allowing the professional thesis typist to produce the high-quality final product.

For those who want to hire a professional thesis typist, the next section deals with how to locate one.

## Dos and Don'ts

Do:

Get a copy of the university guidelines and correct style manual.

Determine whether or not you (or spouse/friend) have the skills, time and equipment.

Confer with a professional thesis typist to make sure you can avoid any obvious problems.

Determine if the added stress from typing the thesis yourself (or having your spouse/friend do it) is worth the savings.

Don't:

Allow yourself to be talked into having a nonprofessional do the job if you feel insecure about it.

Consider just the financial aspect of it — you many end up paying to have the job re-done, and that will cost in both time and money.

Make this decision lightly!

## How to Find a Typist

Referral is by far the best way to obtain information on a thesis typist. Some people/places you might get referrals from are: the graduate office, your department chairperson, your department secretary, your thesis committee members, a friend who had a thesis typed and was pleased with the results. Other sources are library copies of theses (the acknowledgments page), secretarial services (from the telephone book Yellow Pages), bulletin board notices or newspaper ads. The latter methods of obtaining typist names vary in their reliability. Before beginning a discussion of the pros and cons of these methods, please note: some of these sources may not be available at your university; you will have to find the best sources available to you.

*Graduate Programs Office.* Many universities keep a list of names, addresses, and telephone numbers of typists. Sometimes the type of equipment and other services (editing, copying, graphics) are included. Do not interpret the listing as an endorsement — universities usually do not screen typists to see that they meet university standards. The list is simply presented as a service to the student. Ask the personnel in the graduate programs office if the typists have been screened. Sometimes the graduate office staff will even tell you which typists produce the best work. In this case you know the work will meet university standards. Don't be surprised, however, if the personnel refuse to get involved in recommending typists, or if the university doesn't keep a typist list.

*Your department chairperson or secretary.* Your academic department may keep a list of typists who have done acceptable work. You can ask which people are best; however, the personnel may not be able to give you that information.

*Your thesis committee members.* Since these faculty members see the work of typists all the time, you may be able to get a good lead from them. Sometimes professors like a particular typist's work and will refer their students exclusively to him/her.

*Friend's recommendation.* If you have a friend/acquaintance who just completed his/her thesis (especially if the work was done in your major department), and was pleased with the typing job, you can get a valuable recommendation based on first-hand knowledge of a typist whose work met university regulations.

*Checking library copies.* This can be a very time-consuming way of finding a typist because most students do not name their typist on the acknowledgements page. However, if you can't get a name anywhere else, this method does work. Once you find a thesis with a typist acknowledged, check to make sure the work is of high quality. Next, you can try tracing either the typist's name or the student's name in the phone book to see if either can be reached. It is a long shot, not to be attempted unless all previously-mentioned methods fail to produce a typist.

*Secretarial services.* Researching this source produces mixed results. You can find both poor and excellent typists; typists who do and do not know university regulations; good and poor equipment; and higher rates than normally charged by thesis typists. In short, check the agency out *carefully* and ask for references of previous *thesis* clientele. Also, *get in writing that they guarantee their work will be accepted by the university,* and find out their policy on changes and corrections.

*Bulletin boards/newspaper ads.* This is the last choice in finding a typist, simply because anyone can place a notice on a bulletin board or take out a newspaper ad. As a general rule, people who advertise by these two methods are expecting to get term papers to type, not theses. If they specify thesis typing, be sure to ask for names of previous thesis clients and check out their work. Also, be sure to learn the quality of the equipment they use, and make sure it meets university standards. Be careful when interviewing the person to determine whether your typing needs are greater than the typist's experience or ability.

If you're wondering why this stress is placed on finding a "good" typist for a "simple little thing like typing a thesis," the following example provides a reason:

Julianne gave her typist the rough draft of her thesis and went on vacation — without completing the end of her last chapter. To complicate matters, Julianne was at the end of her seven-year deadline and had to complete the thesis within one week or she would not be allowed to graduate. The student had not given a number where she could be reached. Luckily the typist was acquainted with the personnel in the graduate programs office, and she explained the problem to them. She suggested that the typed thesis be logged in and the student be allowed to finish the last few pages upon her return. The graduate office agreed to this proposal, although it was an unorthodox solution. Upon returning, Julianne finished the last chapter and submitted everything for binding. Without the resourcefulness and good reputation of the typist, the student would not have graduated.

## *Dos and Don'ts*

Do:

> Try to find a typist who comes highly recommended by someone familiar with the work.
>
> Determine whether you need a special skills typist.
>
> Request references and check samples of work if the typist you contact has *not* been recommended by someone familiar with the work.
>
> Check out requirements for typists who are put on a thesis typing list — are they screened or added just by requesting it?
>
> Make sure the typist is familiar with your university guidelines and the required typing manual.
>
> Hire a typist with previous *thesis* typing experience.

Don't:

> Get frustrated if you hit a few blank walls in inquiring about thesis typists, keep searching — you *will* find one.
>
> Get discouraged if you hear horror stories about poor typists — the person who had the bad experience might not have checked the typist out thoroughly beforehand, or the student might have been at fault.
>
> Believe that anyone who can type is a thesis typist.
>
> Believe that anyone who advertises typing services can produce an acceptable thesis.
>
> Expect that all qualified thesis typists can do technical typing and graphics.

## *Long Distance Typing*

What if you live far away from the university when your thesis is ready for typing? Many students reside close to school while they are completing their coursework, and then move away while finishing their research or thesis. When the time comes to have the final typing done, they face the dilemma of hiring a typist close to the school or close to where they live. There are some pros and cons to either solution.

If you hire a typist who lives close to the school, you have the decided advantage that the typist knows the university regulations and possibly can work with your advisors to make changes and meet your deadline. The typist may also have established a personal relationship with the graduate office staff. The negative side is that your input to your typist may be somewhat limited. However, if your typist is well qualified and your rough draft is in good shape, the transaction can be successfully handled by mail! If you decide on a long-distance arrangement, be prepared to pay a substantial deposit at the beginning of the work, to be credited against the final bill. The typist may waive this request if you have good personal references, or if you are willing to sign a formal contract.

If you hire a typist who lives close to you, you have the convenience of working together. However, the typist may not be familiar with your university regulations. Also, if the committee or university wants changes made after the final typing, mailing the copy back and forth could result in problems meeting the deadline. If your rough draft is not in good condition, though, you may want the luxury of working closely with your typist.

Note that location close to the university may not be so critical if you live in a large metropolitan area. For example, a student living in the San Francisco Bay Area is within an hour's commute of many colleges and universities, as well as a number of private schools and institutes. Typists in metropolitan areas with many schools can be expected to be familiar with the requirements of many schools and style manuals. Once you have ascertained which typists are qualified to work for you, location may be the determining factor. You may want to find the typist closest to a particular freeway interchange, parking lot, or transit line. This may not be the case if you are from a less heavily populated area with few schools, where typists may tend to specialize in the requirements of a particular university.

It is possible to have successful transactions completed either way. IF the student is specific and organized, and the committee members are willing to assist when necessary, any problems can be overcome. However, responsibilities of all parties must be clearly stated to avoid duplication of effort, and to prevent a last-minute scramble if no one handled some important detail.

## Dos and Don'ts

Do:

Determine whether your rough draft can be typed without a lot of explaining or deciphering on your part.

Decide whether you can expect your committee to work directly with a typist during your absence.

Discover whether you will have more peace of mind knowing your typist is near you (if you provided all materials pertaining to your university requirements) or near your university.

Make sure your typist is a qualified *thesis* typist, because you have the special "distance" problem.

Communicate specific details to everyone involved in the processing of your thesis — if you are absent, they need to know exactly what you want and what they are supposed to do.

Explore the possibility of returning to the university for a short time to complete the submission process.

Don't:

Expect everyone to read your mind — you must communicate exact details.

Be upset if you have to revise deadlines — more time may be needed when working by long distance.

Worry. It is possible to have everything go smoothly even if you are not at the university — if you are thorough, organized and communicate well.

## Selecting a Typist

If you are able to get the names of more than one typist, don't hesitate to call each one and ask your list of questions. You will find that rates and services vary, so you will have the opportunity to select your typist according to what is most important to you — cost, skill, experience, equipment, and so forth.

Your initial phone conversation with a prospective typist is very important — it will give the typist a first impression of you, and you will get a first impression of the typist. Before placing the call, be sure to get organized so you can exchange the necessary information. Make a list of questions you want answered and write down the information you want to give the typist. Then you won't forget anything, and you can compare the answers given by several typists to determine which best fits your needs. Your list should include these questions:

1. What type of equipment does the typist have? Check your university requirements; but it is recommended that your typist use an electric typewriter with carbon tapes and a correcting device. If the typist has a word processor, find out if the printer and paper will meet your university's requirements.

2. Does the typist provide supplies (paper, typing ribbons, etc.)? Most typists provide all supplies, unless your university requires a particular brand of paper.

3. Has the typist worked with thesis/dissertation students from your university in the past?

4. How long will it take to complete your thesis? For this question to be answered you will need to accurately describe your draft so the typist can estimate its length and complexity. The typist will need to know approximately how many pages need to be typed and if there are special time-consuming typing requirements such as extensive tables.

5. What are the rates? How are they calculated? Are there any separate or hidden charges (like fees for conferences or computer memory storage)?

6. Does the typist guarantee the work will meet your university standards?

7. How does the typist handle corrections/revisions?

8. Can the typist provide references from former clients? This is particularly important in the absence of specific recommendations by someone who was pleased with the work.

During your interview, notice such things as: Does the typist seem businesslike, competent, confident, organized and knowledgeable about the thesis process? Is the typist straightforward when discussing rates, corrections, and time requirements? You need to provide the following information:

1. How many pages (approximately) is your thesis?

2. What form is it in (elite type, handwritten, tiny margins, cut and-pasted, have inserts within inserts, or clean-typed with a few revisions)?

3. Do you have special typing requirements, such as tables/figures/graphs, foreign language, mathematical typing? (See Chapter 10, "Graphics and Special Typing Needs.")
4. What is your anticipated delivery date to the typist, and when is your submission deadline?
5. Do you expect the typist to do anything besides type (edit, correct spelling or grammar, alphabetize your bibliography, run errands)?

Once you have exchanged all the necessary information, you will be able to tell whether the typist can deliver an acceptable final draft of your thesis by the deadline. You many want to check references or compare prices. If so, be straightforward and say so. Even if you decide to have another typist do your work, be courteous and let the typist know not to expect your work.

If you are satisfied the typist can meet your requirements without further checking on your part, make a booking for an approximate block of time (i.e., "around the second week in February," the exact time and date can be arranged later). Don't assume that the typist you have selected will reserve a block of time for you unless you are specific in your request. Typists receive many calls of inquiry; some of them result in a thesis to be typed, and the rest don't.

Your next contact with the typist (hopefully) will be when you have approval from your committee members to get the final typing done. ("Hopefully" because in some cases students expect to finish during a particular term, and actually graduate as much as two years later.) If you know you are *not* going to graduate on time, advise your typist to reschedule you for another term. This courtesy on your part will allow the typist to work for someone else in your previously-scheduled time slot.

Neil did not inform his typist that he would be graduating one semester after he had anticipated. The typist was expecting his work, and turned down other typing jobs because Neil's manuscript would be extremely lengthy. When Neil finally was ready for typing a semester later, he called the typist to set up a delivery date; however, the typist had booked other students and could not handle his work. She had already lost business the previous semester because Neil did not keep her posted, and was unwilling to put herself under extreme pressure because he had not informed her in advance of his updated plans. Neil had to search for another typist.

Marty had booked a tentative delivery date with a typist. It turned out that a series of events (faculty member going on sabbatical, death in family, and having to get a job) delayed the delivery date by two years. He periodically called his typist to reschedule new "tentative" delivery dates so she could revise her typing schedule. Marty expressed embarrassment over the rescheduling, but the typist assured him *many* students have to change their schedules because of unforeseen problems. She told Marty she appreciated his keeping her informed, so she would not turn down other work that she would now have time to type. Marty felt better knowing that other students had similar problems.

## *Dos and Don'ts*

Do:

Get organized and write down specific questions you want answered before contacting a prospective typist.

Write down information the typist will need (size and condition of the draft, due date, possible delivery date).

Inform typist of any special requirements (single spacing, tables, figures, technical typing, foreign language).

Note whether the typist seems businesslike, competent, confident, organized and knowledgeable.

Determine whether the typist can meet your deadline.

Call other typists if you want to compare rates, qualifications, or any other requirements.

Advise the typist if you decide not to use his/her services.

Set an approximate delivery date if you feel the typist is the one you want to hire.

Call to set a definite delivery time once you have final approval of the rough draft.

Keep typist informed of changes in delivery dates (including if you are going to graduate a term late).

Don't:

Expect a typist to be able to give you information on typing unless you can provide specific details on size, special requirements, and due date.

Expect a typist to reserve time for you unless you clearly
make such an arrangement.

Hire a typist you are unsatisfied with.

Be embarrassed to call a typist back if you plan to work
with someone else — the typist simply needs the information to plan a work schedule, and will be grateful
that you had the courtesy to call.

Expect a typist to meet an agreed-upon delivery date of the
final product if you do not deliver on time, and you are
not reasonably accurate regarding the amount of work.

## Agreements and Responsibilities

Before discussing conferences between the student and typist,
we offer some common ground rules that will be helpful in making
your agreements. Many problems (and time/cost) can be avoided
with a clear understanding of your respective responsibilities.

*Producing a "true" copy.* The typist is expected to produce an
exact copy of the draft submitted by the student. This includes in-
suring the document adheres to details of the appropriate format
and mechanics of neatness, spacing, and general appearance of
the final copy. It is the student's responsibility to structure the
document in the proper format, and the student is responsible for
content. The student is also responsible for proper spelling, punctuation, and capitalization. The typist may call to the student's attention an obvious case of misspelling, which may be a
typographical error on the draft.

*Proofreading.* The typist is expected to proofread the typed
copy before returning it to the student, and to correct any
typographical errors. It is the student's responsibility to thoroughly
proofread the document both before submitting it to the typist (to be
sure that all notations and changes are clear) and after it is typed (as
a final check on both writing and typing).

*Format.* It is the typist's responsibility to type the manuscript
according to the guidelines for margins, spacing, paragraph inden-
tation, and other physical requirements of the style manual and the
university regulations, regardless of whether these rules have been
followed explicitly in the draft. It is the student's responsibility to
provide the appropriate style manual and university regulations, so
the typist is informed of typing requirements.

*Word divisions.* Word divisions should be held to a minimum. The responsibility of proper syllabification for hyphenated words lies with the typist. However, the student should note whether any words hyphenated in the draft are to be hyphenated when they appear on one line (such as "post-test").

*Equipment.* It is the typist's responsibility to maintain the equipment such that it can produce a clean and acceptable final copy. The typist must also determine before beginning typing if the equipment is able to produce final copy that conforms to the requirements of the university. The typist is expected to use the correct paper quality.

*Time/Cost.* It is the typist's responsibility to explicitly outline the charges for typing and the method of calculation of charges, the time schedule, and any other factors which may affect the time/cost of typing. It is the student's responsibility to provide the typist with an accurate description of the manuscript and any special needs on which the typist will base charges and time estimates.

*Corrections.* It is the typist's responsibility to correct typographical errors in the final draft. The typist cannot be held responsible for errors resulting from illegibility of the draft, or for errors contained in the draft which were copied in the final product. As part of your working arrangement, the typist may be asked to make additional corrections/revisions as requested by the student, committee, or university. This additional work is beyond the scope of your original agreement, and charges for it should be negotiated separately.

*Delivery.* It is the typist's responsibility to complete the typing assignment within the time frame agreed upon. If unable to do so, the typist must notify you so other arrangements can be made. It is the student's responsibility to describe the draft accurately so the typist's time estimate is reasonable, and to deliver the draft on time.

These ground rules may seem elementary, but in practice they can be areas of dispute. Let's discuss their application to your special needs.

Do you want the typist to provide non-typing services (i.e., obtaining signatures, mounting photographs, copying, submission to the university)? This is common when students live out of town or are working full time. If so, discuss your needs thoroughly—and discuss fees. Some typists are not interested in providing such services at any price. A typist working full time at another job may not have the time. However, a typist working near campus may be willing to use a lunch hour for errands. Be specific about your needs. Ask what the typist charges for non-typing services.

Samantha was near the deadline for thesis submission and asked the typist to provide a lot of extra services which she could have performed herself. One of the "extras" she requested was a lot of "whiting out" of black lines and smudges on over 100 photocopied pages in the appendix. The whiting-out process took several hours. When Samantha noticed the charge on the bill she complained that she could have done it herself. When she was told the amount of time involved in the white-out process she understood. Samatha had not considered the amount of time involved in the simple procedure she requested her typist to perform.

If the typist is to produce the final copy by your agreed deadline, you must deliver it on time — all of it! You may want to avoid time and deadline problems by delivering the thesis chapter by chapter. Discuss this with your typist, who may or may not be agreeable to this arrangement, depending on the typing schedule. However, consider that you are relying on your typist to keep everything consistent within your thesis. The best way to guarantee that is for the work to be typed without interruption. If the progress of work is interrupted by the passage of time or intervening work, the train of thought on your manuscript will be broken. Your finished product may not be as polished as you would like. If you want the typing done on a piecemeal basis, you will have to assume the final responsibility for consistency within the document.

Melody had arranged for the typing of her thesis, and had requested to deliver it chapter by chapter instead of in its entirety. The typist agreed to this arrangement since the student had a very large thesis with complex tables, and final approval would not have been obtained until just before the deadline for submission. The piecemeal method would allow completion of the project by the deadline without being under a lot of pressure, and she could also work for other clients. The typist did, however, request Melody be responsible for consistency of format within the thesis, since the typist would not be able to keep a clear train of thought when doing the work intermittently. The student agreed to check carefully for consistency in the rough draft. In fact, Melody ended up bringing the typing a few pages at a time, and the typist worked on it over a period of four months — never seeing it all together. However, the student made her deadline and was pleased with the final product.

In the interest of accuracy of the final copy (and of the time/cost estimate), *your rough draft must be readable.* This does not mean you have to retype every page that has changes. It does mean all changes should be legible and clearly marked. If you have deleted portions of the work, mark clearly which portions are deleted and where the typing begins again. Inserts should be clearly marked as inserts, and typed or written neatly. The exact place of insertion in the text should be clearly indicated. If the insert is on a separate page, place it *after* the page where it is to go. Before turning over the draft to your typist, read it again to be sure all your inserts, deletions, arrows and other instructions are clear. And number the pages!

Kristin presented a rough draft to her typist that was quite messy. There were many inserts, and scribbling throughout the text. But the worst problem was that some pages were not in order, and the draft was not page numbered! Kristine was not available for consultation, so the typist had to search through 150 pages in order to locate the ones that were out of order. She charged Kristin for her time.

Wanda provided an extremely poor quality rough draft to her typist. There were illegible corrections, inserts without clear notation where they belonged, and numerous sections to be omitted in the final typing. After struggling through it, the typist felt she had done a good job. Wanda, however, was unhappy with the work. The typist had repeated paragraphs several times throughout the text. Upon examination of the rough draft the student realized *she* had not gone over her work carefully after her "cut and paste" job; paragraphs were left in which Wanda had intended to remove. The typist has simply reproduced the work as it was given to her.

This is by no means all there is to say about making your draft readable. To keep from getting too far off the topic of agreements and responsibilities in this section, the discussion here is limited to a few general comments. The appendix includes a detailed list of things to watch out for when preparing your draft for a typist. Following those suggestions will be a valuable aid in reducing errors and eliminating wasted time and extra expense in preparing your final copy, as well as making your typist's life easier.

If you want editing, either minor or extensive, or if you want no editing at all, discuss it with your typist. Even though a typist is required only to produce a clean copy of the draft, many typists will routinely correct spelling and punctuation. This constitutes minor editing. If you want no changes, be specific. If you want the typist to correct spelling and punctuation, determine beforehand if there is a charge for that service. Note, however, that if there is a spelling or punctuation error in the draft, and the typist does not correct it when doing minor editing on a "correct as you type" basis, the error is still the student's responsibility. You cannot avoid your responsibility for accuracy of the copy by saying "check the spelling" to your typist. If you feel the manuscript needs a separate and more thorough editing, discuss it with your typist to determine her qualifications and charges (after obtaining your committee's approval). (Editing is discussed in depth in Chapter 6, "Writing, Editing and Proofreading.")

It is advisable, although not required, that you keep a copy of the rough draft, including any changes incorporated into the copy you have given the typist. This is especially true if your rough draft is not neat, or you live some distance from your typist. If the typist has any problems, you can deal with them over the telephone instead of having to meet with her again (which is time-consuming for both of you.)

*Charges and payment* also need to be discussed before the work begins. The typist must clearly outline the charges, based on the student's description of the manuscript. The typist should prepare an itemized invoice of typing charges, and will expect to be paid upon delivery of the typed thesis to the student. If you want to make other arrangements, the time to do so is before the work begins, not when the bill is presented. (This topic is discussed in more depth later in this chapter.)

Penelope had gone over all payment requirements with the typist during the initial phone conversation and again when the rough draft was presented to the typist. However, when the bill was presented she did not want to pay in full. The typist explained that she could not release the work without payment in full, and she would have to hold the thesis until the student brought her a cashier's check or cash.

*Dos and Don'ts*

Do:

Keep your typist informed of schedule changes.

Expect the typist to meet the agreed-upon deadline if you deliver work when promised and your estimate of the amount of work required is reasonably accurate.

Page number the rough draft.

Accept responsibility for accuracy of the draft you give the typist.

Keep a copy of the draft you have given the typist.

Discuss in detail any special services you want the typist to perform (running errands, copying, paste-up, etc.), and expect to pay for those services.

Decide beforehand if you want editing; be specific on instructions to typist.

Pay promptly and in full when you pick up the thesis; if you have special circumstances for payment discuss them with the typist at the beginning of the contact.

Expect the typist to correct typographical errors in the final copy.

Don't:

Expect your typist to sort through the pages to determine where to put the inserts — that's your job.

Expect to deliver the thesis a few pages at a time or chapter by chapter without approval of typist in advance.

Expect the typist to retype pages and make changes required by you or your committee free of charge.

*Conferences with Your Typist*

Once you have selected a typist and have committee approval of your rough draft, the next step is to meet with your typist. You will have to see your typist at least four times: initial delivery of thesis, pickup of final typed copy, return of work for corrections/changes, pickup of changed copy. Extra appointments may be necessary for delivery of additional information or changes required by the graduate office personnel.

The following guidelines apply to all meetings with your typist.

1. Arrange an appointment *in advance* and *arrive on time.* If you are running late, call to advise the typist — the appointment may need to be rescheduled to avoid conflict with another appointment. If you are working with a typist who maintains an office outside the home, find out the business hours. Place your phone calls and arrange meetings within normal business hours, unless the typist is willing to make other arrangements. If your typist works at home, scheduling may be more flexible, but don't take advantage. Find out your typist's working hours and when you may call — some typists work until midnight, while others don't want the phone to ring after 9 p.m. Be considerate of your typist's effort to balance work and family life.

Clarissa was extremely busy with her job and the final completion of her dissertation. Since she was so pressed for time, she never bothered calling her thesis typist before arriving at the house. Clarissa showed up at 7:00 a.m. on a Saturday morning, waking the typist (and her baby); she also wanted to make deliveries as late as 1:00 a.m. Clarissa did not stop to think that the typist had a life apart from typing the dissertation. The typist finally had to tell the student *never* to show up without an appointment, and that her business hours were 9:00 a.m. to 9:00 p.m.

Justin had an appointment with his typist for 7:00 p.m. to deliver his thesis for typing. He did not arrive at the appointed time, nor did he call. Finally at 9:30 p.m. he arrived, telling the typist he had "run into an old friend" and they had a beer together before he came to her house; he "knew she would understand." She informed him she did not understand and that in the future she expected him to call and reschedule if he could not make an appointment.

2. Prepare a list of items you want to discuss with the typist (including a list of page numbers to refer to in the text if necessary), so all your questions can be answered.

Numerous changes were made in Monte's rough draft before it was approved for final typing. He did not retype any of the pages, so there were inserts and handwriting throughout the draft. In several places he needed the typist's advice on the best procedure to follow. Monte did not prepare a list of items he wished to discuss beforehand, so when he met with the typist he had to search through 200 pages of text, trying to locate the questionable areas. The typist had another appointment scheduled 30 minutes after Monte's. When the second student arrived the typist met with him while Monte tried to organize his questions.

3. If you have children, try to arrange for babysitting for the time you will be with your typist. The children may distract your attention from the business being discussed. If you must have children accompany you, bring books or quiet toys to occupy them. Don't expect the typist to provide entertainment for your children; also, if there are no children in the same age group as yours in the house, it may not be "kid-proof."

Alexander's three-year-old son was curious about the "typist" his father was meeting, so asked to go along. Alexander knew his son was quiet and that a book would occupy him during the meeting, so he agreed. After introduction and a few minutes of conversation, the child sat down on the porch and read his book while Alexander and the typist concluded their business uninterrupted. This father knew his son could entertain himself so there was no problem.

Valerie was unable to obtain a babysitter, so took her children to the typist's home. The children were super-active and constantly interrupting. One child wanted some juice, the other wanted to explore the house. (The typist was childless, so could provide no entertainment for the children.) After a disastrous twenty minutes of running after the children, cleaning up spilled milk, cleaning up a broken planter, the business (?) was finally concluded. Several phone calls and another meeting were necessary to adequately answer all Valerie's and the typist's questions.

4. Don't over-stay your welcome. Remember, the typist is running a business. Being friendly and cordial is *great*, but watch for signals from the typist that the conversation is ending.

## Dos and Don'ts

Do:

Arrange an appointment in advance and arrive on time.
Call if you will be late or must cancel.

> Prepare a list in advance so all your questions can be answered.
>
> Arrange for babysitting, or provide a quiet form of entertainment for your children if you must take them with you.
>
> Make all changes in the rough draft *before* delivering it to the typist.
>
> Leave promptly when your business is concluded.

Don't:

> Arrive without an appointment.
>
> Expect the typist's home to be "child-proof" or that toys will be provided to entertain your children.

## Typing/Approval Time Line

A previous section mentioned getting your draft to your typist in time to make your deadline, but more needs to be said about that part of your planning. Working backwards from the graduate office or department submission date, how long will your thesis take to type, and how much time do you need for approval of the final draft?

The answers to these two questions will tell you when you need to have it ready for the typist.

When talking with your typist, try to describe your draft as accurately as possible, in terms of length, condition and complexity. This information is necessary to estimate both how long it will take to type and how much the final bill will be.

Students can't be expected to know exactly how much a thesis will "grow" when final-typed, but there are some guidelines for estimating:

1. Even a clean-typed rough draft can expand by 15 to 25% when the required space is left for margins, headings and paragraph indentations.

2. If you used elite type (12 spaces per inch) and it must be typed in pica (10 spaces per inch) count on a 25% expansion rate.

3. If you have considerable single spacing, advise the typist. She will take that into consideration when making an estimate.

4. If you used tiny margins, count on a 25% expansion.

5. Typing technical information or tables and graphics takes longer and is more expensive than text typing.

Your typist will be able to estimate the number of pages your thesis will be when finished, divide it by the number of pages usually typed in a week, and give you a reasonably accurate time estimate. For example, if you have 75 pages, all double-spaced except the bibliography, you can estimate a 25% expansion rate ( + 19 pages), for a final product under 100 pages. If the typist completes 100 pages a week, you can expect the typing will take about a week. On the other hand, if you have 75 pages total, but 25 are large tables (the typist may consider each table equivalent to three pages of double-spaced typing), and 25 pages are single-spaced (each equivalent to two double-spaced pages), you will have the *equivalent* of about 175 double-spaced pages — about two weeks of typing time. This analysis applies to the cost estimate also, because the final bill will be based on finished typed pages, not on the number of pages in your draft. Being realistic in assessing the size of your draft will allow you to develop a reasonably accurate estimate of how long it will take to type and how much it will cost.

Hector requested that his 100-page thesis be typed in a week. Since this was within the typist's normal workload, she agreed. The student failed to point out that 25 of the pages were thesis text, and the other 75 pages were single-spaced lesson plans (the equivalent of 150 pages of double-spaced typing). He also failed to mention the rough draft was in elite type, and he had left tiny margins on all four sides of the page. By the time the thesis was put in correct format, it expanded about 50%. Instead of contracting for a 100-page paper, it turned out to be the equivalent of almost 250 pages. The typist was under extreme pressure to meet the deadline she had agreed to, and Hector was astonished to see the final bill. [Hector should have related the exact nature of the work; however, the typist erred in not asking for more details before accepting the job.]

After determining how long the typing will take, you need to allow time for each step in the following chain of events:

1. proofreading (usually a student can do it in a day or two);

2. reading by professors/department (this can vary from a day to a week for each person, depending on work schedules — however, it will be *your* job to gently prod them along so they finish in time for you to meet your submission deadline);

3. corrections (the typist will need anywhere from a few min-

utes to a couple of days, depending on workload and number of changes required);

4. graduate office checking of thesis (usually a day or two, depending on how many are submitted to the office—check with them *in advance* to get a time estimate);

5. typist makes corrections requested by university (again, a few minutes to a couple of days, depending on number and type of corrections);

6. copying (your schedule will determine this, but most students can get it done overnight);

7. final submission to university (one trip to campus).

A couple of notes: Don't expect miracle performances from typists. Requesting three hundred pages to be typed in a week (including tables, figures, and graphics) is not reasonable. Even saying, "I'll pay extra if you meet my deadline" won't help. If your request is within the typist's normal output, it will be done anyway. A typist can push and possibly double output for a day, but the risk of errors is far greater. The time gained by fast typing may be consumed in more time spent proofing and making corrections.

Your typist may be able to get help from another typist with a matching typewriter, depending on the condition and typing needs of your paper, and on how busy the backup typist is. This should be attemped only if you are under *extreme* time pressures, and it would be best to have the typist make arrangements with someone he or she has worked with previously.

In short, your typist and committee members can probably be counted on to put in extra effort to help you meet your deadline, but don't rely on it to make up for lack of organization on your part. Graduating a term late may be preferable to rushing your thesis, if you have that option.

## Typing Charges

Now we get down to the question you've been waiting to ask: How much is this going to cost me? Charges will vary, depending on where you live, the subject and condition of your manuscript, and many other factors. Below are some guidelines on determining fair rates and using price as a criterion in choosing a typist.

*Rates.* You will need to shop around to get an idea of the typing rates in your area. For example, in the San Francisco Bay Area in

1983, rates ranged from $1.00 to $3.00 per double-spaced pica page, with the price variation attributable to skill level, equipment and location, as well as other factors. The person quoting the $1.00 rate might have a portable typewriter with a reusable ribbon, cannot do technical typing, and takes a month to type 100 pages. The $3.00 rate may be for typing on a word processor or an electronic machine with memory. Thesis typists with correcting typewriters charged $1.50–$2.00 per double-spaced page.

If you find more than one typist who can meet your needs and there is a $.25 per page difference in rates, your inclination might be to go with the lower rate, but you need to explore this further. What type of machines do they use? Who provides the supplies? Are there charges for corrections/changes? Here are some examples of how typing charges can be determined.

1. *Page Rates*

Typist A charges $1.50 for any page inserted in the typewriter (even if only a page number is added). However, only $1.50 is charged for pages with single-spaced quotes and footnotes. If the finished product is 100 pages long, the bill is always $150.00 — no matter how much work was done on the project. (This pricing would penalize a student who had many appendix pages needing only page numbering; however, it would be good for someone with footnotes and long, single-spaced quotes.)

Typist B charges $1.75 a page, but pro-rates what is on the page (i.e., ½ page is ½ price, ¼ page is ¼ price, one page of single-spacing is $3.50). The typist itemizes charges on the bill, listing page prices from $.25 through $3.50 — depending on the amount of work on the page. This is more complicated, but no students are penalized — they pay for what they get.

2. *Corrections*

Typist A charges $.25 for any corrections that are not typist error. The typist and the student determine whether the changes/corrections were caused by the typist, the student, the student's committee members, or the university graduate office. (Only typist errors are corrected free of charge.)

Typist B does not charge for corrections that can be made without retyping, but does charge for retyping caused by changes made by the student or the thesis committee members.

3. *Supplies*

Typist A requires the student to pay for supplies. If the student does not bring his/her own paper, $15.00 is added to the final bill.

Typist B provides all supplies *unless* the university requires a specific brand of paper, in which case the student is asked to provide the paper.

4. *Booking Fees*

Typist A charges a "booking" fee at the time a student arranges a projected delivery date ($25.00 for up to 150 pages, $50.00 for over 150 pages). The fee is applied to the final bill if the student delivers the thesis near the original date set. However, if the student arrives at a much later date, or fails to show, the money is forfeited.

Typist B does not charge a booking fee, but tells all students that the theses are typed in the order they come in. The typist's advice to students: Call me when it is ready for delivery and I'll guarantee it will be typed within one to two weeks.

As you can see from these varying policies, it is important to find out exactly how a typist determines the bill before deciding that $1.50 a page is cheaper than $1.75 a page. In the instance cited above, the $1.75 page rate is probably the more economical. Also, you must take into consideration the typist's reputation and guarantee of the work. If you have technical work, and the slightly higher-priced typist comes highly recommended by your department, it may be worth your money to pay the higher fee. (The price difference on a 100-page paper is only $25.00, but it could pay for itself in less production time and/or fewer corrections.)

If your work requires extensive tables, graphs, figures, charts, or technical/chemical formulas, it is highly advisable to pay the fee for a good technical typist and/or graphic artist, unless you have the ability to do it yourself. Your typing could be very expensive — plan on it in advance. In determining fees for such highly skilled work, the typist usually times the work and charges an hourly rate. Hourly rates for thesis typing are usually based on the page rate. For example, if the typist charges $1.75 per page and averages 10 pages per hour, the hourly rate will be about $17.50. If you prefer a page rate for technical typing, the typist can calculate it — again based on the standard page rate and how long the technical portions take to type. Following the above example of $1.75 per page and $17.50 per hour, if the typist can only type two pages of complex equations per hour, you may be quoted $8.75 per page; three pages per hour would be about $5.80 per page.

The point is that you are paying for the amount and difficulty of the text, balanced against how long it takes to type. Under these

circumstances, it would be better to get a typist who does this type of
work frequently, so will be fast and accurate at it, rather than hiring
a less skilled person who may charge less per hour, but will take
longer and may make more mistakes.

*Payment.* Your agreement with the typist on charges and
method of payment should have been made before the work began.
When the work is ready, the typist should let you know the amount of
the bill. Confirm at that time whether payment is to be made by personal check, cash, or cashier's check. If cash is requested, don't be
offended or assume that the typist is cheating on taxes. A request for
a cashier's check is usually precipitated by a run of bad luck with
personal checks. No matter how you pay, you should receive a typed
bill explaining the charges. If you pay in cash, the typist should sign
the bill and mark it "paid."

Keep your receipt! In some cases the expense of typing a
thesis/dissertation is tax deductible. Check the Internal Revenue
Service regulations. If your employer or someone else is reimbursing
you, they will want documentation of the cost.

*Discrepancies.* If there is a discrepancy in the bill, don't panic!
Check the bill when you get it, or when you get home. If you have
questions about some of the charges or find an error in the bill, let
your typist know. There are two kinds of problems here:

1.  If the typist made a *calculation* error the overpaid funds
should be reimbursed immediately.

2.  There may be a discrepancy between what the student and
typist feel the charges should be (especially when special services are
provided). If you disagree with the charges, discuss it with the
typist. If you have a valid complaint the bill may be adjusted; or the
typist may feel the bill is correct. If that is the case, the typist should
explain the bill to you so *you* understand it. However, talking about
it will allow you to air the situation and come to a mutual
agreement. Some examples showing different outcomes will shed
some light here.

Troy felt he had been overcharged for special services provided by the typist. He discussed the bill with her, and it turned
out what was really bothering him was that the bill was so large.
He had anticipated spending about $150.00 for typing and the bill
came to $250.00. The typist pointed out there had been a 30%
expansion of the original work, and that the bill included typing
25 pages of detailed tables, in addition to the special services he
requested. Troy had not taken into consideration the expansion of

text, and when the typist told him the amount of time she spent on the tables and errands he felt the bill was extremely fair (in fact, Troy offered to pay an additional fee). The typist refused the extra money, saying that the initial bill had been correct.

Wilma made arrangements for her thesis to be typed. However, she ran into problems with committee approval, and was forced to call her typist and postpone the typing. By the time Wilma finally obtained committee approval and called her typist to arrange a new appointment, two quarters had passed and the typist had raised her rates. When Wilma saw the final bill, calculated at a higher page rate than she had been quoted, she questioned it. The typist realized her agreement with Wilma had been made at the earlier page rate. She honored the original agreement and recalculated the bill.

Jill arranged for typing of a final draft of her thesis. When it was finished, Jill proofread it, noted corrections, and asked the typist to make copies and mount and label figures. When all the work was done, Jill reviewed the bill and paid it by check. Later, Jill called to complain about the addition of four hours of labor at an hourly rate, in addition to charging for the copying. The typist explained that the hourly rate was based on what she would have made if she had been typing during the time it took to run the errands, and produced receipts showing that the charges for copying were accurate. Jill still felt the bill was too high, and stopped payment on her check. After trying unsuccessfully to resolve the matter, the typist finally took it to small claims court. Jill had to pay the full bill plus court costs.

*Alternative methods of payment.* If your budget is so tight that you cannot come up with a large sum of money to pay a typist, discuss it openly and at first. Some typists are willing to extend credit, others are not. Some typists will release work that is partially paid for, while others will hold it until final payment is made. A successful solution might be for you to start making monthly payments at the time of initial contact, so some of the bill will be paid upon completion of typing. If the typist does agree to time payments, make your payments promptly. Complete honesty about your financial situation from the outset is of extreme importance if you need special favors regarding payment of your bill.

Oliver knew that typing his dissertation was going to cost several hundred dollars, and he did not have the funds to pay that amount in one payment. He also knew the typing would be done over many months. He explained his financial situation to the typist in his initial phone conversation and asked to discuss it in detail when they met. Oliver offered to pay $100.00 a month during the time the typist was working on the dissertation, and $100.00 a month after it was completed until the bill was paid off. The typist was impressed with Oliver's honesty about his financial situation, and also that he agreed to start making payments immediately instead of waiting until the project was typed. She agreed to his proposal. As it turned out, since he had made payments each month while the typing was being done, he owed very little when the project was completed.

Your typist may also be receptive to other methods of payment—the barter system still does work. This is where spouses and families can help, too. We have known typists who traded their services for:

•honey and other produce from a farm owned by the student's family;

•the student's services in setting up an accounting system for the typist's business;

•the student's wife sewed a full cover for a sailboat the typist and her family owned.

The barter system is a valid method of payment, but it will work only if you have a service or product to offer which the typist needs. Its success also depends on the two people involved. If you have any doubts that you will be able to follow through with your part of the bargain, that the typist will follow through, or that this will be an exchange of equal value, don't attempt a barter arrangement. If you agree to an exchange of services, you may wish to include a backup agreement—for example, preparing a bill which the other party should pay in cash if the service to be rendered is not completed within, say, six months. Don't be offended if the typist refuses your offer—equipment must be paid for and other financial obligations may require cash. (Other methods of paying for typing and costs of graduate school are discussed in Chapter 15, "Grants and Other Sources of Funding.")

## Dos and Don'ts

Do:

Find out the going rate for typing in your area.

Find out exactly how the typist determines charges.
Find out who provides supplies (typist or student).
Take into consideration the quality of the work produced
and the typist's reputation.
Hire a technical typist/graphic artist if your work requires
it — it could save you money in the long run.
Pay promptly in the manner requested by the typist.
Check your bill.
Discuss any discrepancies on the bill with the typist and try
to come to an agreement if you feel you were unfairly
charged.
Discuss any time payment request with the typist during
your initial contact.
If the typist agrees to time payments, keep your part of the
bargain and pay promptly when the bills are due.

Don't:

Assume a cheaper base rate will cost you less.
Assume corrections/changes are free — check with the
typist for policy on determining these charges.
Expect the typist to provide services at a cut rate or free of
charge.
Expect your typist to release your work if the bill is not
paid — discuss this in advance.
Make any assumptions about charges for extra work not
included in the original workscope.

## Breakdowns

If you hire a reputable typist, and things are going smoothly, is
there a chance something can go wrong? YES!
1. Your typist can get sick and end up in the hospital.
2. The typewriter can break down or the word processor can
have a memory failure, forcing a halt for anywhere from a day to a
week (depending on how reliable the repair service is).
3. Urgent business (death in the family, etc.) could take your
typist out of town for a week.
4. Personal problems can interfere with a typist's production
schedule.

The point is that things can and do happen — you are employing a *human being*. Even the most reliable of typists can occasionally have personal or mechanical breakdowns that interfere with the production schedule.

You can help safeguard against such occurrences by checking the reputation of your typist regarding past performance, ability to meet deadlines, and quality of work produced. Does the typist have a reputation for bad health, or is a lot of work turned over to a second typist for completion? Is over-booking of typing jobs common, or failure to meet deadlines? This information will let you arrive at some conclusions regarding the typist's work planning and reliability.

Another approach you can take is to ask how the typist would solve specific problems.

*Question*: If you get sick, what happens to my thesis?

*Answer #1*: It will still be there to type when I am well, but don't worry, it will get done — even if you miss your deadline and have to graduate a quarter late.

*Answer #2*: My husband and two friends are also thesis typists, and their typewriters are the same brand as mine. If we get into a jam, I can subcontract the unfinished project to one of them if your deadline is approaching before I am well enough to resume work.

*Question*: What if your typewriter breaks down?

*Answer #1*: It should be repaired within a week.

*Answer #2*: I would be willing to rent a machine if your deadline is too close for comfort.

As we've said before, we're not trying to scare you — just help you be prepared if something goes wrong. These things don't happen frequently, but they *do* happen. Make sure you have a typist who is prepared to deal with them!

If your typist is unable to finish your work on time, it may be possible to arrange for another typist to take over. Graduate office personnel may be sympathetic and, if the delay is not long, you may be able to arrange an extension of your deadline.


## Turkey Typist

After all your research and checking around, you finally selected a typist who appeared competent to meet your requirements and whose price sounded reasonable. And the product was not

acceptable. The first question to ask is, did you supply all the information the typist needed to meet the requirements, and deliver a
readable draft? If you did and the typist still used the wrong
margins, wrong paper, incorrect or inconsistent format, poor
quality equipment, made unacceptable corrections, didn't finish on
time, what do you do?

First, ask the university to provide a list of reasons why the
work was unacceptable. If possible, ask your typist to correct/retype
it. The typist may be willing to retype your thesis, and still meet
your new deadline. If you undertake a retype, you must carefully
determine whether the typist can or will do it and what, if any, additional charges will be involved.

If the typist was never qualified to do the work, for some reason
is not willing to make it right, or is not willing to work with you on
it, you will have to try to get your money back and find another
typist to retype your thesis.

The original typist has three choices: (1) return your money,
(2) refuse to return the money, or (3) compromise and return part of
the money. The typist may be willing to return your money if you
show the list of reasons why the work was not acceptable, and return the typed copy.

The typist will probably be unwilling to refund all your money,
since time, effort, and supplies were expended on typing the thesis.
You can try to compromise, if you feel comfortable paying a portion
of the bill for something that was rejected. If so, you need to do some
clear-headed negotiating.

If you're unable to reach an agreement on a partial refund, or if
the typist is unwilling to make any refund, you can either drop it or
take the typist to court. If you decide to drop it, you can go back to
the source of the referral and let them know that your experience
with this typist was unsatisfactory.

You may decide to pursue the matter as far as small claims
court. You must weigh your chances for success against the time
commitment of preparing a court case. Your typist may produce a
refund when a summons demonstrates that you are serious.
However, the typist may feel he or she is the wronged party, and
may be as anxious as you are to see the matter resolved in court.

It is important to keep all documentation and evidence to build
a strong court case. You will need to take a prepared statement of
the facts as you see them, the typist's bill, your proof of payment of
the bill, the finished thesis, the university's (and/or your new

typist's) list of reasons why the first copy was unacceptable, and any other documentation and exchanges of information you had with the typist. If you do not have a written agreement with the typist, don't worry—verbal agreements are also binding, although more difficult to substantiate.

You may find the effort in preparing a court case worthwhile, even if you don't win. It is an educational experience. If you do win, you may be able to get your money back, although small claims courts only render a judgment and do not provide for collection. With the judgment in your favor, however, your typist may refund your money, or you may turn it over to a collection agency.

In the meantime, your deadline is approaching and there is still the matter of your unaccepted thesis. With this history of typing problems behind you, the university graduate office or your department may be willing to make a recommendation or help you find a reliable typist. You may still be able to meet your deadline. It is important to remember not to duplicate mistakes made with the first typist with the second, and that this is an entirely different arrangement. Do not expect your new typist to make up for your problems with the first, although the typist may be sympathetic and put in extra effort to help you meet your deadline. The new typist may also be willing to prepare a list of reasons why the first version of the thesis was unacceptable, to strengthen your court case.

You do not have to accept the work of a turkey typist. Hopefully, you will have taken the time to select a reliable typist; but in the event you end up with an unacceptable product, don't give up. There are several avenues of recourse. The object is, after all, to finish and submit your thesis.

## Conclusion

Your relationship with your thesis typist can be a rewarding professional experience or it can be a complete disaster. As you have seen in this chapter, a large part of the outcome depends on you. Typists appreciate students being prompt, courteous, organized, and considerate. They have served as advisers, encouragers, counselors, sounding boards to bounce ideas off, as general facilitators, and as rooting squads for their students. Some of the experiences lead to friendships as the thesis typist watches the growth of students through different phases of academic and professional careers. If you build good rapport, you can use your typist's services in future work (resumés, applications and letters to prospective employers or graduate schools, dissertation typing, journal articles, and maybe even typing a book from your research).

Students appreciate typists doing a good job on their theses and meeting their deadlines, and show their appreciation in varied ways. Some students send "thank you" cards, flowers, candy, wine, or bonus money. But the best way they can reward a typist is by telling their faculty members and other students about the fine job the typist did for them — leaving an avenue for future referrals.

## Chapter 8
# Word Processing

The rapidly expanding computer age has made the magic of word processing readily available to the general public. There is a degree of mystique to word processing, because a slightly higher level of training is required to operate a word processor than a typewriter. There is also an element of status to having your thesis done on one. However, you must determine whether a word processor or a correcting typewriter will best meet your needs.

If you're considering word processing for your manuscript, you must first answer some basic questions:

1. What is it?
2. What are its advantages/disadvantages over a correcting typewriter?
3. What are the additional costs, if any?
4. Will my university accept the final product produced by a word processor?
5. Do I need it?

The purpose of this section is to give you some background information to help answer these questions and decide whether you need or want to use word processing instead of a correcting typewriter for your manuscript. No attempt will be made to go into an intricate explanation or comparison of different systems or programs; however some advantages and disadvantages will be presented.

## What Is It?

Word processing is, simply, computerized processing of text. It allows revisions to the text without complete retyping, and printing is automated.

The first draft is typed into the computer memory and displayed on a CRT (cathode ray tube), or screen. The text can then be revised, paragraphs moved around, and major or minor editing performed before the text is printed. Format can be changed with a few keystrokes, and subsequent revision can be accomplished with minimum retyping.

Every word processing system has six features in common:

*Keyboard.* Much like a normal typewriter keyboard, although it will have additional special-function keys. "Keyboard" and "input" are also verbs, to mean the act of typing on a word processor.

*Monitor.* The CRT or screen, which looks something like a TV screen, on which the text is displayed.

*Memory.* The most common information storage medium is floppy disks—thin, flexible disks of mylar, either 5-¼" or 8" in diameter, protected by a square paper jacket.

*Disk drives.* The "box" which houses and reads the magnetic disk, allowing the typist to store and retrieve information.

*Printer.* The device that types your words onto paper.

*Software.* The set of instructions (program) that tell the computer what to do. In a dedicated word processor the word processing instructions are built in; in a computer with word processing capability, the word processing instructions are a separate program from the computer system's operating instructions.

## Advantages of Word Processing

1. After the initial typing, corrections and revisions may be made with minimal time investment.

2. Proofreading subsequent drafts is simplified because you only have to carefully check the *new* material—the older text has not been altered. If you elect to read the entire draft after revision, an error-free final copy should result.

3. The text material is stored in the computer's memory. If some disaster should befall your copy, in any draft stage or after the final is prepared, another final copy may be produced quickly and easily. (This may involve arranging with your typist for extended storage of the document, and may involve extra charges.)

4. Storage of the text material in the computer's memory makes it easier for you to rework the document into an article, series of articles, or book, for publication elsewhere.

5.  Working through multiple drafts on a word processor requires establishing a good working relationship with your typist. Your typist can do the work you need quickly and efficiently, eliminating the time you would need to spend orienting a new typist for each phase of the post-thesis work.

6.  If you need multiple drafts of your manuscript, word processing will prove to be cost-efficient because of the automated printout and limited time required to make revisions.

7.  Some software will "search and replace." This allows the typist to locate all occurrences of a word or phrase and correct or replace it. For example, if you want to make sure a term is correctly spelled (did you use absorption and adsorption correctly?) you can check each occurrence of the word. Or if you've decided to use one reference instead of another, you can locate every mention of Smith (1981) and change it to Jones (1982). Having the machine do the searching is more reliable than doing it manually.

## Disadvantages of Word Processing

1.  Word processing usually costs more than typing on a typewriter, either as a higher page rate or as a set-up charge. The equipment has higher initial cost and overhead, and is therefore more expensive to operate. Additional operator time is also required to format the machine to the specifications for your manuscript. If it turns out that you have organized your writing well and have no major revisions, you will have paid more for your first (and final) draft than you would have with a standard typing.

2.  Data stored in one word processing system may not be readable by another machine that is not a duplicate of the first. Unless your typist has a system with multi-user capability, the option of having more than one typist work on your manuscript at the same time may be eliminated or restricted.

3.  If you don't get along well with your typist, it is more difficult and costly to change typists in midstream than if the document were just typed on sheets of paper.

4.  If the system "goes down" (loses its memory or otherwise doesn't function), you can lose valuable time. A matching computer/word processing system may not be as easy to find as a replacement typewriter would be. If the disk itself is damaged, everything stored on it may be lost. However, it is possible for the

typist to make a duplicate [backup or safety] file on another disk to minimize the loss if this should happen.

5. If the capabilities of the word processing system (or the typist's ability to use it) have been misrepresented, trouble can arise after you've made a considerable investment in time and money. This can also happen if you have not been clear in specifying your requirements. For example, if you said "project," the paper quality may not be important, and the kind of paper the typist's printer can handle may be adequate. However, if it's really a thesis, the printer paper may not be acceptable.

## Neutral Areas

1. The document must be keyboarded (typed) at least once, whether by typewriter or word processor. The efficiency and accuracy with which this can be done depends in part on how well organized you are.

2. The need for careful proofreading remains, whether the document is produced on a typewriter or on a word processor.

3. Technical typing is also "neutral," because whether it's more suitable for typewriter or word processor depends on (a) how technical, (b) the capability of the machine, and (c) the capability of the typist.

Either machine, *properly equipped*, can type equations, foreign language, scientific notation and other special needs. On a typewriter, type fonts may be changed quickly and easily, and a half-space ratchet for consistency in equations is now standard on most machines. The capacity for multi-level equations depends solely on the typist's ability.

Word processors present different problems in reproducing technical typing. The machine can do only what it is programmed to do, and is then instructed to do by the typist. It has to be told to superscript or subscript, and the printer has to recognize that command. If you have no equations in your manuscript, but use notations like $H_2O$ or $CO^2$, or if you have footnotes, they present no problem on a typewriter. But if the printer is not capable of a reverse half-line feed, it cannot type even these. It is possible to leave a space and insert the numbers manually, but that takes time and defeats the purpose of automated typing. If this capability is important in your manuscript, you must state your requirements clearly and be sure your typist and the equipment are capable of meeting them.

## Other Things to Think About

Whether you need or want word processing depends in part on your writing style, your subject, and the extent of revisions you anticipate will be required by your committee members — the great unknown.

Marissa's drafts had been returned by her committee members with so few notations she was beginning to think they had not spent much time on the chapters, or even read them. She was investigating a new field of study, so had expected more feedback. Marissa's precaution of having her thesis done on a word processor turned out to be warranted, because her committee members waited until they had the final copy in hand to make substantial revisions.

Kyle felt his thesis was in good shape, but was nervous about changes and revisions his committee might request. There had been some internal bickering among his committee members during the course of his research, and many changes had been made on his handwritten, early drafts. Kyle contracted with a typist who offered word processing, anticipating a fair number of changes from his committee.

As it turned out, his committee members had made all their recommendations during the course of his work, and approved his thesis with only minor revisions. Kyle felt the word processing investment had been worthwhile anyway, as an insurance policy for his peace of mind.

If your text is going to require more than one draft or if you anticipate extensive revisions from your committee, it may be worth having your work put into a word processor. The time and cost savings for production of a second draft would be considerably less than having a thesis retyped. Any higher initial cost per page or per hour will average out, getting progressively lower with each succeeding draft.

If you are very organized and what you put on paper is pretty much what you want to say, and if you anticipate the revisions will be minor or well-contained, a typewriter will do the work at as high a quality and a lower cost.

Generally, you should consider word processing if:
•English is not your first language;
•your committee members have a history of disagreement over the content, direction, or wording of your manuscript;
•your committee members have not seen a complete typed or very clearly handwritten draft;
•you are a doctoral candidate;
•you plan to rework the document for publication in a journal or for another use;
•your rough draft is in such poor form that a typist will have difficulty figuring out what you intended to write.
•you are writing the manuscript in pieces, and may make inserts into "complete" chapters.

Only you can make the decision which method to use. Take all available data into consideration: the cost, your committee, your subject, your level, your writing style, the shape your draft is in, the capabilities of your typist.

If you contract for word processing and find you don't have to do enough revision to justify it, you still have the resource to use in rewriting your thesis or dissertation for publication or to use as a base for future research. Or you may decide it's like an insurance policy, which you pay for and may not need, but are thankful for if you do need it.

## If You Decide on Word Processing

As with everything else in your graduate career, your success depends partly on how well you communicate. Here are some areas unique to word processing you need to investigate and clarify with your typist:

*Format.* The recording of margins, tab stops, printing details, page length, and other instructions regarding the appearance of a document. (In this context "format" can be seen as a verb; in its usage as a noun, "format" is the set of general requirements for the physical appearance of the document.) Word processors format a document according to preset "default" specifications unless instructed otherwise. In some systems this includes a justified (flush or even) right margin. Some systems print in several type sizes, including proportional. Make sure your typist knows the university requirements so the document can be formatted properly. It is *your* responsibility to make sure the final copy meets all your university standards.

*Printer.* Many different kinds of printers are available for word processors, the major two types being dot matrix and full-character. Dot matrix printers create letters formed of groupings of dots in the shape of a character. The quality is steadily improving, but even at best dot matrix output can not be mistaken for letter quality. Full-character printers, often referred to as "letter-quality," produce print like a typewriter. Dot matrix printers are usually much faster than letter-quality printers, and your typist may use one for rough drafts. However, this is one case where close is not good enough, so insist on a letter-quality printer for the final draft.

*Paper quality.* Some universities require submission of the original typed copy on a specific type of bond paper. Make sure the word processor can handle the paper requirements. Some can use cut bond paper, others can't. There are many variations on this theme:

•If the printer can't feed cut bond paper, and you plan to do enough drafts to justify using word processing, you can hire someone else to type only the final draft on a typewriter, using the type of paper your university requires. This will cost extra for the final typing and will require additional proofreading, but you will have saved money on all the rough drafts.

•Your school may accept the new "razor cut" computer paper — a good quality bond with serrations so close together they are almost imperceptible.

•Some universities require submission of a copy on bond paper, but don't require that it be the original typed version. Then you can have the word processor print on any kind of paper, and have the copies photocopied onto the required bond paper.

•Some schools want a clean original typed copy, but have no paper regulations. The best thing to do is take a sample of the paper to the graduate office or your department and ask if it's acceptable.

*Storage.* One of the advantages of word processing is memory storage of your document. Your typist may: (a) charge a flat rate for storage, depending on the length of the document; (b) store it free as a service, whether you request it or not; (c) routinely dump the file after the printout or after a fixed amount of time, unless you specifically request that it be stored; (d) store your document forever, but require that you pay for the floppy disk it's stored on. Find out your typist's policy on memory storage, and make your agreements before the work is undertaken. Remember, it takes only a second to dump an entire file, but once it's gone, it's gone. If you have made the investment in word processing, it may be worth it to pay extra to keep your document on file until the approved, bound copy is safely sitting on the library shelf.

*Cost.* Be sure you are well informed of your typist's charges. Don't hesitate to ask any question — things that seem too insignificant to ask or volunteer at the outset may turn out to be important later on. Find out how much will be charged and how charges will be calculated, how the typist expects to be paid, and if there are any other charges that may apply to you — like set-up, storage, multiple copies, and printout onto cut bond paper instead of tractor-feed computer paper. You should also be clear about what you expect your typist to do. Do you expect an accurate rendition of what you have submitted, or do you want major or minor editing services as well?

*A note of caution.* As you have noticed in the brief discussion of terminology, some words have a specific meaning in word processing that is different from their accepted non-computer meaning. "Edit," for example, is an operating mode in word processing, when the software will allow revisions to a document. This is very different from the "edit" which means to correct grammar and sentence structure. Be sure you and your typist are using the same meanings for words when discussing the requirements of your manuscript.

Since word processing your thesis involves a repeat and sometimes lengthy working relationship with your typist, make sure you establish good rapport. One way to do this is to start researching typists before you need one. Take a term paper or short manuscript to your selected typist and see the results *before* you commit your thesis. Make sure the typist is familiar with the regulations you must meet and the equipment is capable of performing the necessary functions.

Sybil hired a typist using a word processor to work on her master's thesis. She knew she would have three revisions of the draft, and didn't want to spend time typing it three times herself. However, she failed to ascertain if the typist could meet her university requirements. The equipment could not produce a copy that was acceptable to the university, so the student had to hire a second typist to type the thesis on a correcting typewriter. [Had Sybil known the situation at the outset, she might still have elected to use the word processor for the initial two drafts;

however, she would at least have been prepared for having to pay another typist for the final typing. More thorough checking in advance would have saved Sybil much stress.]

The general guidelines for preparing the manuscript for typing (outlined in Chapter 7, "You and Your Typist," and in the Appendix) also apply if your typist uses a word processor. In addition, don't take advantage of the ease of revision available with a word processor. Give your drafts to your typist in as complete and clear a condition as possible.

## Conclusion

As word processing becomes more and more available, university graduate personnel and faculty members will become accustomed to its advantages and disadvantages, benefits and hazards. The corresponding developments in technology have affected typing equipment, resulting in several types of electronic typewriter with limited memory. Whether you need a word processor, or can meet your requirements with a correcting typewriter, will depend on your organization, writing ability, and graduate committee. The better organized you are, the more smoothly the whole process will flow. At a time when you are experiencing mounting pressures from school, committee, family, work and multiple other sources of pressure, you don't need to have things go wrong with the physical production of your thesis. Putting some effort into determining your needs will help prevent problems in this area—don't limit your research to your graduate project!

## Dos and Don'ts

Do:

Realize word processing may cost more initially.
Expect to save money with a word processor if you need two or more drafts typed.
Discuss *all* costs when learning about word processing.
Make sure a word processor can meet university regulations.
Familiarize yourself with word processing language before you see a typist.

Check out features provided by a correcting typewriter.
Weigh advantages and disadvantages of word processor
and correcting typewriter *before* deciding which to use.
Be specific about what you expect from your typist.
Learn what your typist expects from you.

DON'T:

Pay for word processing if you don't need it.
Assume the system can meet your needs without checking
it out.
Presume storage is available and/or free—discuss this in
detail with your typist.
Expect your material to be stored indefinitely—arrange a
"dump date" or pay for your own disk so you can have
it stored for a long period of time.
Presume your typist knows your university requirements—
make them available.
Hesitate to ask questions!

Chapter 9

# Revisions

This chapter deals with a topic that causes many students headaches, heartaches, frustration, confusion — in short, induces the feeling of "I don't want to continue." Even if everything up to this point has gone smoothly, you WILL have revisions. How many is too many, too few? Who makes them? How do you handle them? What exactly should you expect regarding revisions at the master's versus doctoral level? Will you graduate on time? How can you keep revisions to a minimum? Do you pay the typist for revisions? These and more questions will be answered in this chapter.

## *Committee Feedback*

The single most important factors in determining the amount of revisions are the relationships (a) among your individual committee members and (b) between you and your committee. (See Chapter 4, "Committee Selection," for more details.) If your committee members are in agreement on the direction of your research, the revisions should be kept to a minimum. Make sure you solicit feedback from *all* your committee members early in the process, and follow their suggestions. Otherwise you will get their advice at the end — when you will be forced to rework a lot of your thesis. These suggestions will certainly not guarantee approval without changes, but should cut down drastically on the number of revisions. Careful attention to writing style and thorough editing can also hold down the number of revisions you may be asked to make. (Refer to Chapter 6, "Writing, Editing and Proofreading.")

Students' reactions to changes and revisions vary widely:

Vincent had received intitial approval from his committee, so he had his dissertation final-typed. When he took the work to his committee members for their signatures, he was told, "You did a fine job; now we want you to explore a completely different direction." Vincent had spent over $400 on typing alone, and was so discouraged he wanted to quit school.

Yvette did not type, so had her rough draft professionally done. The committee members were completely familiar with her work and she had listened to and incorporated their suggestions. When the rough draft was presented for initial approval, they signed it after suggesting only minor changes. Most of the draft was submitted without retyping. Yvette graduated with few problems and saved considerable typing expenses.

As these examples show, committees vary and so do students. The one thing to remember here is that it is *your* project, so do not lose control over it—keep it moving. When your committee members suggest changes, make them if at all possible—and do it promptly. If you feel something is unreasonable, talk to the other committee members for a consensus. But do try to incorporate most of the suggested changes. Remember: You need their signatures. It is important to be able to distinguish between changes that must be made, those that are only suggestions, and abstract doodles in the margin.

The number of changes you can expect will depend to some extent on the feedback you have received throughout the research and writing process. If you have been in constant touch with your committee members and have already incorporated their suggestions, there may be few changes in the final stages. If your committee members are doing all their recommending at the end, expect considerable changes. With luck, the bulk of the changes will be made *before* you pay for typing. *Do not get discouraged with this process*—every student goes through it! If you find you are getting stagnated, talk with other students in your program—try to form a rap group or confide in a particular friend. If nothing else works, call your typist to chat about your problems. Finding out someone is rooting for you can make a big difference in your outlook! (See Chapter 11, "Stress.")

What constitutes too few changes? If you feel you don't want to make *any* changes, you've probably made too few.

How many changes are "too many" depends on you. If you reach the point where you want to discontinue the program, you may need to step back and take an objective look at your work. Talk to your committee members. They may be able to (a) give you the encouragement you need to complete the project, or (b) make concessions on their changes. But TRY to bear with them and make as many changes as you can. This may require some super-human diplomacy on your part, particularly if your committee members are making contradictory suggestions. You may have to help them to communicate better with each other. It may require asking your department chairperson or a respected faculty member for help. (Go back to Chapter 4, "Committee Selection," and read Amber's story again to reinforce this point.)

There is a definite difference between what is expected at the master's versus the Ph.D. level.

*Master's level.* As a general rule, at the master's level students get considerable feedback throughout the formative period. They can expect that, as they submit their initial proposals and individual chapters, the committee members will suggest changes. They may tell the students to go in new directions, expand or shorten an area, or point out that a certain area has been entirely omitted. They may tell the student to write in past tense instead of present tense. But in general, the *major* portion of the work is usually accepted.

Although master's students often experience frustration and feel they are being required to do a lot of extra work if substantial revisions are required, the master's program generally runs smoothly for an *organized* student.

*Doctoral level.* Many doctoral students do not get considerable feedback at the early stages of their research. This may be partly due to their advanced learning level, and also because they have usually done research before. Other doctoral students get continual feedback throughout their program. (This depends on the needs of the student and the committee composition.) However, doctoral students should be advised: *do not expect your initial "final" typed copy to get approval — even if you have a verbal okay before you submit it to your typist.*

Since the doctoral work is viewed as the "final" educational experience, the last pre-professional growth period, it will be handled as the last great learning opportunity. Such instruction as "You did fine; but now I want you to go in this new direction" should be expected. Experience has shown that many doctoral candidates submit *three or four* entirely *different* final products before they obtain their degree. Many doctoral students miss their initial deadline and have to completely revise their schedules.

How do you best deal with this?

1. Expect it from the beginning. This will allow you to make a reasonable time line, and you can continually update it. It will also decrease your frustration.
2. Actively solicit your committee members' advice throughout your graduate work. This could cut down on changes later.
3. Seek support from friends in the program. They are all going through it too, and mutual airing of feeling can provide much needed moral support.
4. If you need money, you *can* work while completing your dissertation — in fact, it may greatly relieve the pressure you might otherwise feel. But remember, always keep working on the dissertation. Don't drop it completely or you may never get back to it.

Finally, a student whose master's thesis was approved with little revision may be surprised to find approval of a doctoral dissertation much more difficult. It is not unusual for the standards against which a dissertation is judged to be more stringent than thesis standards — particularly at a university that offers both degrees. (See Chapter 2, "Planning Your Program," for further discussion.)

## Student Changes

You will want to produce a high quality manuscript; therefore, extensive editing changes will be made from the first draft to the final copy. You need to obtain a copy of a style guide to get specifics on the format; you might also want to obtain a copy of a writing guide. The standards for a thesis are higher than for term papers or a senior project. It's not difficult, but does require that you be thorough in your organization. (See Chapter 6, "Writing, Editing and Proofreading.")

You will be incorporating changes suggested by your advisors; you may also want to solicit advice from friends in your field. One note of caution — you can get too much helpful advice. Your paper can become someone else's pet project. Whether friend, mentor, student, or advisor, watch out for inappropriate suggestions. It is your thesis or dissertation — weed out suggestions that can shift your paper away from the topic you intended.

Woody's draft was approved, and he had taken it to a typist. Woody then began to nervously question the quality of his work, and sought advice from his advisors, past professors, and friends. He needed their acceptance of his scholarship and talent. It was suggested he rewrite parts that had already been approved, delete some sections, and expand others. Woody's subject had been properly presented, but now his findings and discussion wandered from their course. In trying to please everyone, his time frame got completely away from him. He spent long, exhausting hours rewriting. He delivered pieces of his thesis to his typist as he rewrote. In Woody's case, lack of confidence led him to too much unnecessary guidance and help.

Finally, let go of your work once it is in the typist's hands.

Heidi's committee members were satisfied with her work, but she could not quit working on it. After promising it to the typist by a certain date, she turned it in two weeks later—one chapter at a time. As each chapter was being typed Heidi was revising the next. She missed her submission deadline, so felt she should continue to change things that had already been typed. In all, about one-third of the thesis was retyped, and Heidi graduated a semester late.

## Time Line Problems

What if you miss your graduation date? Revise your time line to reflect your new goals. (See, in Chapter 2, the time line section.) At the Ph.D. level this occurs regularly. Do not let it discourage you to the point of interfering with completion of the dissertation. Keep the project moving! Thousands of master's and doctoral degrees are awarded each year, and not one of them was easy!

## Cost for Changes

How much you will have to pay for changes is something you must iron out with your typist (preferably at initial contact). Charges vary, as shown by these examples of typist policies:

1. Typist A charges 25¢ for every correction, plus normal page rates for retypes. Charges are levied even if the error is the typist's fault.

2. Typist B charges by the hour for any corrections that are not typist error. (Fault is verified.)

3. Typist C charges only for changes that result in retyping a page.

4. Typist D records the amount of time it takes to make corrections/changes, assumes one-half the errors are the typist's and the other half are the student's, and charges by the hour for the student's half of the errors.

A good guideline would be: expect to pay for any corrections/changes that were not the typist's fault. Such errors commonly result from unreadable handwritten copy; technical terms misspelled in the draft; poor quality of the draft, such as cut and paste, multiple insertions, or poor photocopy quality; non-English text (either foreign language or technical). (For more details on typist charges, see Chapter 7, "You and Your Typist.")

You may wonder why, after paying a healthy sum for typing, you should pay for corrections/changes. The answer is simple. When contracting for typing, you are purchasing a service that involves the typist's time, effort, equipment, and supplies. When the initial bill is paid, you have settled for the services *already provided*. Any extra work required will utilize additional services, which should be paid for (except correction of typist errors).

One other major point to consider here is pressure on the typist. You are trying to meet your deadline. The typist is trying to meet your deadline. The typist might also be working for other students with deadlines. (It is not unusual for a typist to be working with four or five students at one time.) To meet these deadlines, the typist needs your cooperation in being as accurate as possible in your work and instructions, and in noting changes/corrections as requested.)

An important note: Be very careful to follow your typist's instructions in noting where changes and corrections are to be made. The method can vary greatly. For example, if the document was produced on a word processor, the revised pages will be reprinted, so the typist may want the changes marked on the typed copy in red ink so they are easy to find. If the document was produced on a typewriter, marking on the pages may mean that some would have to be retyped that otherwise could have been fixed with the correcting device. The best way is to note changes on a separate list.

Otto was a chemistry major. His thesis contained chemical equations, which required extensive technical typing and drawing. When he proofread his thesis after the final typing he disregarded the typist's instructions for notation of changes. Otto wrote in a hard lead pencil throughout the text. In order to meet university correction standards the typist had to retype every page on which he had noted changes. Although Otto willingly paid for the retypes, the typist was under extreme pressure to meet his submission deadline.

The time needed for corrections can vary from the same day to a week or so, depending on how extensive the changes are. (But don't expect to wait for them.) When you take your corrections to your typist, have your list checked and request a time estimate. (Point out any *major* corrections specifically.) This will allow you to plan the final steps in the graduation process (obtaining signatures, copying, submission to the university).

Another caution: Don't let the original typed copy out of your hands except to have a circulation copy made. You may be willing to follow your typist's instructions for noting corrections, but your committee members may not be. Invest in an insurance copy. Your committee members of course have to have the original approval page, but they rarely need to see more than a copy of the thesis itself. Many otherwise perfect pages have been retyped (at the student's expense) because they came back from committee review stained with peanut butter, coffee, grease, pawprints, handprints, stray doddles, blood (paper cuts are common), or looking like they'd been retrieved from the wastebasket. The extra copy also keeps you from fainting when the professor returns it with a note, "Good work! It is all there except for pages 22–37, which I seem to have misplaced." Or from wanting to kill when you are told, "I've signed your thesis, but have temporarily misplaced it. It's probably in the back seat of my car ... or maybe in my den with the graded final exams. Don't worry, it will turn up."

Randall's business dissertation contained 25 intricate tables which had taken hours for the typist to prepare. The graduate committee members decided they wanted an extra table added, thus changing the table numbers for tables 18 through 25. Instead of noting the change in pencil, or simply preparing an instruction sheet to that effect, one faculty member wrote the new table numbers on the original copies in marking pen. Marking pen cannot be erased. The university required submission of the original tables and did not allow white-out. The eight tables had to be retyped, at the student's expense. [Had no marking pen been used, the typist would have been able to change the table numbers using the typewriter correction device.]

## Conclusion

As you can see from the discussion, you should expect considerable changes in your manuscript — particularly if you are a doctoral candidate. Try to incorporate as many of the suggestions into
the work as possible. Working closely with your [carefully selected]
committee members and typist will help minimize revisions. DO
NOT count on getting signatures until you have them — even if you
have verbal approval of your rough draft.

If you find yourself getting bogged down, talk to your committee members and to other students in the program, or seek moral
support from rap sessions. Don't get discouraged — the students
before you survived, and so will you.

## Dos and Don'ts

Do:

Expect to make revisions.
Work closely with *all* your committee members
throughout your research and writing process.
Incorporate as many committee suggestions as possible.
Turn loose of the project once you have given it to your
typist.
Revise your time line if necessary.
Expect to pay your typist for changes.
Have confidence in the quality of your work.
To alleviate stress, seek help from committee members,
friends in the program, and rap sessions.

Don't:

Get discouraged by the number of changes.
Lose control of the project — keep it moving.
Be inflexible.
Expect your typist to decipher the changes for you — you
must do that.
Ignore your typist's instructions on how to make changes
and corrections on the final typed copy.
Circulate the original typed copy.

## Chapter 10
# Graphics and Special Typing Needs

Few theses or dissertations can be prepared for submission without some amount of graphics or special needs typing. Some areas of study are obvious candidates — biology, chemistry, geography, and education use graphs, flow charts, tables, maps and other visual means of presenting data. Even subject areas that are more text-oriented, such as history and English, use maps, flow charts, diagrams and tables. How much technical or graphic assistance you need depends on your topic, and how it is presented. This chapter will help you determine the level of special skill needed to prepare your thesis, where to look for it, and what to expect. Areas discussed include the differences among different kinds of visual presentation, technical/statistical typing, preparation of graphics, foreign language, use of color, finding a special needs typist, time/cost elements, and printing considerations.

## Definitions

Before tackling this technical subject, it's best to get the words defined so we're working from a common information base. The following definitions are grouped so you will be able to spot the differences among the words used in this discussion.

*Visuals.* General term for presentation of data by visual rather than textual means. The same data can be presented several different ways, depending on how much detail is needed and the intent of the visual. Visuals include tables, figures, charts, diagrams, graphs, maps, photos, blueprints, illustrations, and line drawings.

*Tables.* A systematic arrangement of data in a tabular format (columns and rows). Usually numerical, the data can also be textual; the key is that it is arranged in a tabular format. These are properly labeled "tables" and are included as such in a List of Tables behind your Table of Contents.

*Figures.* Symbolic representation of facts in a visual format. This covers the wide range of visuals that are not tables: maps, charts, graphs, diagrams, illustrations, and all their variations. Every visual representation in your thesis that is not a table should be labeled a figure and listed in the List of Figures behind the Table of Contents. Some subject areas use particular types of visuals, which are then labeled by their specific name and included as a separate list. For example, a geography thesis might contain a number of maps, in addition to tables and other types of figures. The maps would be labeled "maps," and a separate List of Maps would be included with the Table of Contents, List of Tables and List of Figures. A biology thesis might include a number of electron micrographs. These may be called "plates" and listed on a separate List of Plates. You must be consistent throughout your own paper, and the visuals singled out for special notation must be appropriate to your field.

*Plates.* Another name for photographs, particularly when they are full-page size or assigned a page with no text on the page.

*Charts.* A perfectly good word but badly treated. *The Merriam-Webster Dictionary* (New York: Pocket Books, 1974) defines chart as follows: "map; a sheet giving information in the form of a table, list or diagram; graph." Because of its broad definition it does not convey enough specific information to be of any value. Charts are appropriate to some fields (such as medicine). If the terminology is accurate, use "chart," but be consistent in labeling. Again, a separate List of Charts may be included.

*Legend.* The title and other explanatory information about a figure.

*Technical.* Any of the fields that comprise the sciences or quasi-sciences, including chemistry, engineering, biological sciences, computer science, linguistics, educational psychology, and others. Some fields use technical language for portions of a report and standard English for the rest.

*Statistical.* A branch of technical, encompassing the narrower field of mathematics and statistics. The difference between the two is that, although both use technical language, the statistical more often includes equations as part of the text. While it is possible for a paper in chemistry, linguistics or biology to be written in text (although it may need special symbols), the math or statistics paper rarely goes more than a page or two without including complex equations.

*Foreign language.* Any language other than standard English; sometimes fields with highly specific vocabulary or terminology (jargon) are considered "foreign," but these are more appropriately termed technical.

*Symbols.* Any letter or type element that is not standard English. In the typing process this requires either changing the typing element or inserting hand-drawn symbols. These include Greek, linguistic, other foreign language, mathematical, musical, and any other special notations used in your field.

*Special-needs typist.* A typist who has skills, training and experience beyond the basic requirements of thesis typing. These may include graphics, editing, technical or statistical typing, foreign language, or a combination. As discussed later in this chapter, you must assess the requirements of your manuscript before you begin looking for a special-needs typist.

*Master.* The original copy of the final-typed document or drawing. The sheet from which all other copies are made.

*Printing.* Mechanical means of reproducing original copies of a master copy. Requires transference of ink to paper.

*Copying.* Reproducing copies of an original by photoreproduction. The resulting prints are not originals; they are copies.

## Doing It Yourself

Your own skill, training and expertise will determine whether you can prepare your own visuals for the final copy of your thesis. Even if you are qualified, you must also consider the time it will take.

You best know your skills and the equipment at your disposal. For example, if you are an accomplished draftsman, producing structural drawings to conform with thesis format requirements would not present a problem. If you took a course in cartography, you can probably prepare all the maps for your geography thesis. On the other hand, if your research is in statistics and you are a hunt-and-peck typist, it would be inadvisable to try to type it yourself. Likewise, if you're a music student but your drawing and handwriting are not the best, it would be better to hire a professional copyist to reproduce the original score for your thesis.

You also need to consider the time required to produce the visuals. It does not take very long to make a pencil sketch of the visuals you need (providing the analysis to produce the numbers is already done). It may take a couple of hours to make a presentation-quality pen and ink final drawing. A computer can churn out pages of printout in minutes, or you can extract the information you need to construct a draft of your table and write or type it in rough form. It takes approximately two to three times as long to type a one-page table as it does to type a page of text.

This is one area where you may wish to delegate the responsibility for final production. Then you can turn your attention to the other details that need your attention — your text, committee, or comprehensive exams.

It must be stressed that if you do the final preparation yourself, it must conform to the university and style guide requirements. You would also be advised to confer with your typist regarding number and placement of the visuals, accurate labeling, and legends.

If you hire the work done by a professional, that person is only responsible for the mechanical details of spacing, neatness, and following your instructions to produce an accurate and acceptable table or figure. While typists and graphic artists may be able to offer valuable advice based on experience, they are not responsible for designing your visuals or for extracting the information or analyzing the data to compile them.

## The Basic Requirements

Visuals increase reader understanding and retention of information by supporting, clarifying and expanding textual points. A table or figure is self-contained, so the reader can stop and study it. Combining text with tables or figures is the most effective method of presenting qualitative data — complex relationships are interpreted, findings are revealed, and numbers take on a clearer meaning. It is also easier to compare types of information or different variables if they are presented in a uniform graphic manner.

If your analysis lends itself to visual presentation, you must decide where, when and how many visuals to use. A final rough draft of your visuals should be prepared before the final rough draft of your manuscript, for several reasons: You need to know what data are presented in each visual before you can discuss it; you need

to know if your visuals are adequately designed or present data
clearly enough before the text is typed, in case you need to make
changes; your visuals must have accurate legends and titles so the
table of contents and lists of tables and figures can be compiled; you
need to know how many tables and figures are being used, and that
each is properly cited and placed in the text, so you don't wind up
with extra or missing visuals.

Keenan had 75 visuals in his Ph.D. dissertation. He labeled
them "figures," although they were a combination of tables,
figures, and graphs. He asked the typist to go through his 350-
page manuscript, re-labeling them appropriately. This also consisted of proofreading the text to change each mention of "figure"
to the new label. The project was extremely time-consuming,
requiring the typist to bill Keenan for many hours of labor.

A good table or figure doesn't try to present too much information. It should contain only one fact or series of facts, and be easy
to interpret. Visuals contribute to your paper by presenting data
that may be too complicated to write out clearly; however, if your
figures or tables are too complex, they may defeat the purpose of
ease of understanding, and two or a series of figures, each concentrating on a fact or two, would be more effective.

It's not necessary to visually present all of the data in your
analysis, nor do you need to repeat in text everything that is shown
in your visuals. If your visuals are well designed, you need only refer
to them, and give enough explanatory information to make the
visual relevant to the text. For example, pie charts are used frequently to demonstrate budgets — where money comes from and where it
goes. "Figure ____ illustrates the school district's budgeted income
and expenditures for the 1983-84 school year," is all that needs to be
said in introduction of the figure, which would follow as soon as
possible in the text. The significance of these figures would then be
discussed. Likewise, "Student council representatives preferred to
allocate additional funds to the child care center instead of the pep
squad, with the voting depending more on age of the representative
than on sex, as had been anticipated (Table ____)." Then the table
would follow, with statistical breakdown showing age groups of
males and females, and how they voted.

Care should be taken in balancing your paper. Don't use too
many visuals, or too few. The guideline on building tables and
figures is that they must be self-contained. The text gives the
reasoning and conclusions; the tables or figures give the specific

numbers or trends from which the conclusions were derived. Use them where they are needed to advance the understanding of your discussion. Note that throughout this book we have used examples of student experiences to illustrate the point being made. Even though these are not numbered, they are treated as visuals in that they are indented and set apart from the rest of the text, thus providing a break from the text and visual treatment, in addition to giving explanatory information.

If you need help in formulating your figures and tables, ask for it. Professors, other graduate students, and university staff members from departments as wide-ranging as the sciences to art may be willing to offer helpful advice; and don't forget about your school's visual aids department. Commercial advertisers, lithographers and printers also can provide guidance and assistance for special graphic needs.

## Titles and Legends

Effective titles for figures and tables are brief and concise. Apply your guidelines for writing a thesis title to captioning tables and figures. The easy way to do it is to ask, "what does this table or figure show?" If that question can't be answered in about one line, there is something wrong with the construction of the visual. It may be trying to convey too much information, in which case maybe two or more visuals are needed instead of one.

If you have a series of tables or figures, let the titles reflect the relationships as well as the differences. The reader should be able to tell from reading the title if this table measures the same groups as the previous one, but includes a different variable.

Table titles are placed above the body of the table. Additional information may be included as a note below the table, together with any footnotes and the source citation.

Figure titles, also called "legends," are placed below the body of the figure. When the figure takes up a whole page or is mounted, such as a photograph, the legend is often placed on a facing page. Information included in a legend is determined to some extent by your field of study; for example, maps must always include the scale, and photomicrographs must always include the magnification. Any data necessary for accurate interpretation of the visual must be included in the legend or notes.

Table I

SAMPLE TABLE

| Stub Head | Box Head | | |
|---|---|---|---|
| | Column Head | Column Head | Column Head (%)[1] |
| Major row stub[2] | | | |
| Row stub | January | .005 | 3 |
| Row stub | February | .013˙ | 10 |
| Subordinate stub | 1-14 | .006 | 4.5 |
| Subordinate stub | 15-28 | .007 | 5.5 |
| Row stub | March | .026 | 20 |
| Major row stub | | | |
| Row stub | Eastern | .35 | 26 |
| Row stub | Western | .70 | 52 |

Source:  The source of data if not from your own research,
or the citation of another document.

Notes:  The levels of heading will vary with the complexity
of the data.  Comments in this section apply to the entire
table.

[1]The percent (%) sign is placed here to eliminate
repetition in the column if all numbers in the column are
percentages.

[2]The major row stub sometimes is centered and
boxed, in which case it is called a spanner head.  Usage
depends on the style guide.

Check your departmental and university regulations for any
special format requirements that apply to your field of study and
thesis topic. Your style guide will also have format guidelines, as
well as examples of titles and various ways of structuring tables and
figures.

Tables present detailed information in a small space. A simple
table can give information that would require several paragraphs or

pages of text explanation, and tabular presentation is often the only way large quantities of individual or related facts can be arranged.

The simpler the purpose and presentation of a table, the better. Each table should be focused on one kind of data or relationship. For example, "Of the 53 students interviewed, 35 (66%) preferred the quarter system, 13 (25%) preferred semesters, and the remaining 5 students (9%) had no opinion," fits smoothly into the text without overloading the reader. If more variables were included, such as sex, age, or class level, tabular presentation would be a more effective way to present the data. A good guideline to follow is whenever the statistical information makes the text become labored or the sentence structure too elaborate, a table is needed. It's easy to lose the reader in a long string of numbers.

If the reader must cross-check information from one table to another, keep the headings, units and column arrangement in the tables consistent.

An exception to the tables-must-be-tabular guideline is made when the information is not tabular, but is arranged systematically. Genealogical tables or formulas of chemical compounds often require special formats.

Some shortcuts can be made to shorten or simplify tables:

•Break long, complex tables into a series of shorter ones focusing on one relationship.

•Shorten numbers by indicating in the column heading that (for instance) all numbers are in thousandths, and then shorten the numbers by the appropriate number of decimal places.

•Note all units consistently used within a column in the heading, rather than repeating it with each number (say "%" in the heading and then list only the digits in the column, rather than having each entry read 14%, 15%, 16%, and so forth).

If your tables must be long, format them so all the headings can be placed on one sheet (sideways if necessary). Then the table can continue for several pages and retain its continuity. If the headings will not fit across one sheet, the table may be reduced to fit within the margins. Care must be exercised when reducing to assure that the reduced table fits within the university margin requirements, and is still readable.

Remember that when drafting your pencil copy of a table it is possible to squeeze a great many numbers onto a page. Translating this to a typed page requires counting the digits and spaces. The numbers may vary according to the margin requirements of your university, but are calculated based on 10 horizontal spaces per inch in pica, 12 in elite, and 6 vertical lines per inch in either size. A typed page has about 48 vertical lines for copy, including any needed for title, headings, and footnotes. A page has 58 horizontal spaces in pica or 71 elite spaces. A horizontal (sideways) table has approximately 36 vertical lines for type, and about 85 pica or 100 elite spaces horizontally. When figuring how much data will fit on a page, be sure to allow adequate space between columns (absolute minimum of two spaces) to assure readability.

Longer or more complex tables can appear in your appendix. These tables usually supplement information already in tables, figures, or text, and will be of a less critical nature. They are often the working data from which the other visuals were drawn. If used, your text should indicate their location ("The tally sheets are included in Appendix D.").

The spacing rules for text tables are usually strictly enforced for those contained in the text, but may be bent for appendix tables. Check with your graduate office to see if you may exceed the margin requirements for tables contained in an appendix.

## Computer Printouts

Once you have a half-inch-thick pile of computer printouts in hand, a symbolic token of all your work as well as the actual representation of your results, the desire to use all of it in your manuscript may be overwhelming. It may also overwhelm your reader. Unless it is necessary to include all the computer printouts (for example, if you're presenting the base data from which your reader is to calculate something), you should carefully select which data to include. The printout may not be intelligible to your readers, and will probably contain more information than you need to include in your paper. (Also consider that if you have to defend your thesis, *any* number or statistic in the output is fair game to the defense committee. Be certain you know the meaning of everything you include.)

After deciding whether all or part of the data are to be included, look at the printout carefully. Is it of a quality that is acceptable? Is it on white paper or on blue- or green-banded paper? What size? Is it readable? Was it printed with a dot matrix or a letter-quality printer? In all likelihood, it will be on 14-inch wide paper, banded, and printed with a high-speed dot matrix printer. This is great for getting fast results to work with, but not of good enough quality to be included in the document. Take the originals and a good copy of them to your graduate office and ask. If the originals can't be used or aren't of good enough quality, the prospect of having all those tables typed is enough to encourage you to carefully reconsider how much of the data you really need to include — only enough to support your written findings.

Tables included in your text must be consistent in format and typestyle. If you have a combination of computer-generated and typed tables, all should be typed for consistency within the document. However, if all your tables are straight off the computer, ask the graduate office if they need to be retyped or can be used as is. If computer-generated, they must still fit within the margins required by the university, or be readable if photo-reduced. They would also probably need to be copied onto the correct paper.

## Dos and Don'ts

Do:

Determine whether you are going to type your tables or have them done professionally.
Introduce your tables in the text.
Research your style book and university guidelines for correct table formulation.
Formulate a table whenever information in text becomes overly statistical.
Use the same terminology throughout your paper's tables.
Keep the titles simple.

Don't:

Ask or expect your typist to formulate tables.
Create tables that duplicate text presentation.
Try to produce your own final tables unless you have the experience and equipment.
Present a table when text presentation will suffice.
Call a table a figure.
Photoreduce the tables so much the type is unreadable.

*Figures*

A figure is a symbolic visual representation of facts. Figures can be line drawings, charts, graphs, curves, or diagrams. They include maps, plates, plans, photographs, illustrations, paintings, blueprints, musical scores, and even some types of computer printouts. A simplified definition of a figure is anything that isn't a table.

Figures differ from tables in that a table presents only one fact or series of facts, while a figure can also present dimensions such as timed relationships between tasks. They illustrate or compare, show similarities or contrasts, and interpret statistics or facts. Each type of figure requires different graphic treatment, ranging from simple figures produced on a typewriter to more complex figures requiring special drawing and other equipment. Even though a figure is more versatile and can illustrate more aspects of the data, it should still be focused on a main theme, with no clutter or unrelated data.

The two general types of figures are illustrations—those requiring some amount of drawing and may contain type—and photographs.

*Illustrations.* Among the figures that are reproduced by some form of drawing are graphs, maps, flow charts, and a wide range of variations. The most common types of graphs are line graphs, bar graphs, and area and volume graphs.

A *line graph* shows the relationship between two variables. Time, age, distance or weight data, for example, can be visualized and compared.

*Bar graphs* contain heavy lines or bars depicting the relationship among certain data or groups of data. Some bar graphs use different lengths of bars to show direct comparison of data, while others have bars of the same length and present breakdowns of data within each bar. The latter is a version of the pie chart.

*Area and volume graphs* show relationships among quantities. The pie chart is a typical example, and is often used to represent budgets—such as the silver dollar cut into pieces to let taxpayers know where their money goes. The "pie" represents the total quantity, and the "slices" represent proportions of that quantity. This is a particularly good illustration to use when one quantity is greater than the others.

Check your style book for other examples of figures. The type best suited to present your data depends on what kind of data you have, and the message you are trying to give your reader. Each type

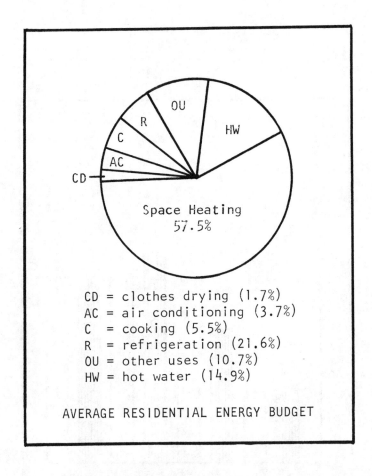

CD = clothes drying (1.7%)
AC = air conditioning (3.7%)
C  = cooking (5.5%)
R  = refrigeration (21.6%)
OU = other uses (10.7%)
HW = hot water (14.9%)

AVERAGE RESIDENTIAL ENERGY BUDGET

**Sample area and volume graph (pie chart).**

of visual has a different impact and stimulates a different response
from your reader.

*Maps* are especially versatile means of illustrating different
types of data in relation to a land mass. The same base map can be
used repeatedly to show vegetation, wildlife, soil types, geological
structure, land use, and all other uses to which land is put. Maps
also show location, distribution, density and arrangement of
phenomena. Each map must show the scale to which it was drawn,
a direction symbol, and its title and legend or key. Maps are
specialized and therefore are not well covered by the style manuals.

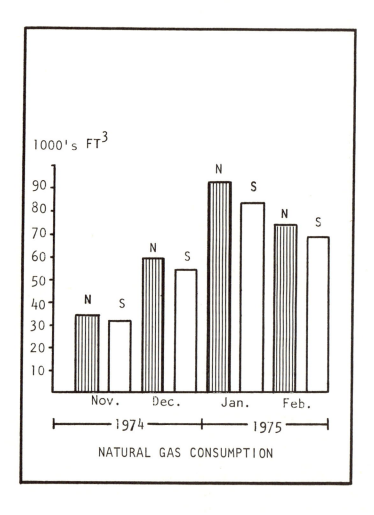

**Sample bar graph.**

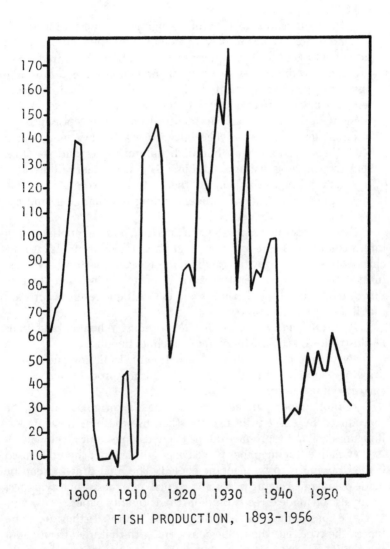

FISH PRODUCTION, 1893–1956

**Sample line graph.**

A good resource book on map presentations is Arthur Robinson's *Elements of Cartography* (New York: John Wiley & Sons, 1978), about $30.

Ula's thesis was a study of changing farming patterns in a specific region. It was important to show how the land use in the same region had shifted over several generations. She hired a cartographer to draw one base map of the region under study, and had copies of the map printed. Each variable was then represented by a shaded area on a copy of the base map. Throughout the thesis were 15 maps, each an identical base map representing a different growing phase. The last was a summary map, again with the same base map but with different lines and shadings showing the progression of land use. The maps clearly illustrated the data without duplicating the text, and were a valuable visual aid to the reader in understanding the changing land use patterns over several generations.

*Flow charts* show a progression from one point to another, with intermediate steps. A computer program is a good example. A flow chart is an effective way to visually reinforce step-by-step directions, instead of taking up several paragraphs of text to instruct, "first do this, then do this, then do that, then do this if one result occurs and that if the opposite result occurs."

*Materials and procedures for illustrations.* When making finals of illustrations, keep the following guidelines in mind:

•Never use pencil, felt pen, or ballpoint. India ink and a good drawing pen will produce an excellent finished product that can be corrected if necessary.

•Graph paper can only be used if the originals are to be reproduced by offset printing, and then use the blue-lined paper. Blue lines will not reproduce on the printed copies, but green will.

•Opaque tracing paper placed *over* graph paper should be used if the drawing is to be machine-copied. The final drawing can be made on opaque tracing paper and copied onto thesis-quality paper. It can also be made directly onto the thesis-quality paper.

•Be consistent in the lettering for the figures. If they are to be typed, the type face should be consistent with that used throughout the thesis. If Leroy or other template lettering, or transfer (rubdown) letters are used, the lettering on all figures should be consistent.

•Be sure that the lettering will still be readable after the figure is photoreduced.

•Figures that contain only black and white, with no shading, reproduce well with good machine copies. However, drawings with shading, such as wash drawings or photographs (called continuous-tone or half-tone copy) do not reproduce well and must be screened.

•Screened drawings and photographs will sometimes reproduce well on a high-quality copy machine.

•Be careful with photographic reduction of graphic materials like maps, where proportions are important. The reduction process can distort the perspective or proportions.

•Folding an oversized map or chart may be preferable to reducing it. If folding is necessary, the first fold should be right-to-left, then top-to-bottom. Take care that the fold is made so that the edge is not slit when the thesis is trimmed at the bindery, or that the loose edge is not trapped in the binding.

•If transfer or rubdown shading or lettering is used on visuals (such as Letraset, Chartpak, Zipatone, Formatt), it is best not to use the original in the bound thesis. Use a good copy as an original. The press-down shading will curl and come off with age, and rubdown letters will dry out and chip off.

•An illustration generated by a computer should be of good, reproducible quality. Make sure the printer is a graphic printer and has a high-quality ribbon. Computer-generated figures must also conform to the margin requirements.

•Take care to assure that the final drawing and any legend material fit within the required margins.

Daphne wanted to save money so told her typist she would provide the final copy of all figures. The student prepared the figures without observing the appropriate margins, and was not consistent in placement of figure captions. The graduate office rejected the figures, and Daphne had to prepare them a second time.

*Photographs.* The other general category of figures is photographs, including blueprints.

*Blueprints* are not suitable for reproduction in a thesis — they're blue. Even if they are reproduced in sepia (brown), they will not make a clean copy. If it is necessary to include blueprints in your thesis, check with the graduate office for their special requirements. Often if the blueprint cannot be rendered in a black-and-white version, an original must accompany each copy of the thesis. If the blueprint is oversized and must be folded, it is usually placed in a pocket in the back of the bound book. Depending on your department and university, and the number of folds required, the blueprint might be included as an oversized figure in the text.

*Photographs* (also called plates) require special treatment. Some universities have requirements regarding the weight of paper the photograph is printed on, in addition to directions for mounting or not mounting. Some, for example, give specific instructions for how to mount the photos, and direct that mounted original prints for each copy of the thesis to be delivered with the typed draft; others specifically direct that no photos are to be mounted until after the book is returned from the bindery!

Check with your graduate office for the preferred mounting procedures for photographs. Do not plan on using staples, paper clips, scotch tape, or photo mounting corners. Rubber cement used to be the preferred mounting method, although after a few years the chemicals in the cement discolor the finish on the photograph. A thin coating of white glue works well, provided the photograph can be kept under an oversized weight until the glue is completely dry, to keep the photograph from curling. The preferred method is to use photographic dry mounting tissue. This is available in photographic supply stores, and many of the stores have dry mounting presses that can be used in the store or rented.

Depending on how many copies are being made, you may wish to have the plates printed separately rather than printing original photographs for each copy of the thesis. This can be done by having a screen or half-tone made of the original print, and having the required number of copies offset printed (see printing and copying section). (A caution is offered not to draw or write on the reverse side of your photographs if using the screen/offset method. The camera will pick up the lines and reproduce them on your copies.) Whether this method produces an acceptable copy depends on the quality and contrast in your original photographs.

If your photographs are in color it will be necessary to have originals made for each copy, since color printing is prohibitively expensive. However, if your university stores the documents on microfilm, the colored photographs will not reproduce and therefore may not be acceptable. Again, check with your university before having the prints made. It is possible to make black and white prints from color negatives of slides, although the quality suffers.

A special note on *photomicrographs*: These elaborate on the text rather than presenting any new data, and should therefore be cropped judiciously and arranged for most economical use of space.

The detail in photomicrographs is of paramount importance, so it is usually best to plan on including original prints in each copy of your thesis, rather than trying to reproduce them as halftones.

Carroll had many plates (photographs) in his thesis, and only one figure. The one figure, however, was simple but important because it summarized the trends of the student's findings. He wanted it to stand out. The typist's suggestion to use color was approved by the graduate office, so the typist prepared the figure using different colored matte tape for the lines on the figure. The copies were made with a color photocopying machine. Enough copies were made to put a color figure in each copy of the thesis. The final effect, as Carroll had wanted, was to make the single figure stand out and to show its importance relative to the photographs.

## Dos and Don'ts

Do:

> Determine whether you are going to draw your figures or have them done professionally.
> Follow university and style book procedures for formulating and producing your figures.
> Follow university and style book instructions for adhering photographs.
> Plan each figure to represent a simple theme.
> Prepare your figures so they are self-contained and understandable without text.
> Introduce your figure in the text.
> Choose the right type of figure to present your data in the most dynamic manner.
> Use India ink and a good graphic pen to produce lines for figures.

Don't:

> Make long titles for your figures.
> Use a felt pen or pencil.
> Use lined graph paper for your final figures.
> Use inconsistent lettering on figures.

Include color photographs in your paper unless approved
by the university.
Write on the back of photographs to be screened and offset
printed.
Adhere photographs with paper clips, staples, scotch tape,
or photo mounting corners.

## Special Needs

Manuscripts with special typing needs encompass those areas
which require special expertise to read or type. These papers require
the writer to pay special attention to style, format and accuracy of
the draft, as well as painstaking proofreading. Preparing the
document may be a monumental undertaking, but correlating it
with complex visuals or assuring accuracy of multi-level equations
demands an even greater level of attention and effort. As the subject
area is more complex or difficult, the typing process is also tedious
and often requires special equipment. Your typist must have special
skills, equipment, and preferably experience in your field of study.

The discussion and guidelines in this section focus on general
categories of special needs, such as technical/statistical, foreign
language, and fields that require special formats such as the fine
arts. Some fields overlap. The guidelines are therefore general, to be
applied to the specific needs of your own thesis.

*Technical/Statistical.* "Technical" applies to any of the fields
that comprise the sciences and quasisciences. These include the
"hard" sciences such as physics, chemistry, and biology, as well as
fields that have technical aspects, such as educational psychology,
business, linguistics, and computer science. The statistical subset of
technical applies to the mathematically-oriented fields. The common elements found in all these areas are technical language, extensive use of symbols, and equations. Numbers and units of measurement expressed in numerical values are common in text, and
symbols and abbreviations are used to an extent in technical manuscripts that would not be considered proper in nonscientific writing.

One of the additional responsibilities of the writer in a
technical field is to maintain consistency throughout the manuscript
in usage of symbols and abbreviations. As an aid to clarity (a road
map) and to reduce the number of errors, it's a wise precaution to
give your typist a list of all symbols and abbreviations. A similar list,

showing meanings of symbols and abbreviations, is sometimes included as an appendix, especially if many symbols are used or the document is lengthy.

This precaution is especially important if your draft or the equations are handwritten, because it is very difficult to tell if a number or symbol is subscripted or superscripted. The list of symbols, however, will still leave questions such as, is "1" a one, lower case L (ell), or should it be a script $\ell$ (ell), often used as an abbreviation for liter? Is "0" a zero or a capital O (oh). Make sure you note the differences between letters that appear similar in English and Greek — a and alpha ($\alpha$), p and rho ($\rho$), t and tao ($\tau$), and so forth. An effective option (or addition) to making a list is to clearly mark all symbols in the text. The extra time it will take to perform this step will pay for itself in reducing the number of errors that must be corrected (and paid for) later.

Quinton's physics thesis was about electronics. Throughout the manuscript was a notation that looked very clearly (to the typist) to be a lower case handwritten "r." It turned out to be an upper case omega. Quinton was angry, and asked the typist, "If you couldn't read it, why didn't you call me?" The typist replied, "But I could read it — it looked like a lower case r. I can't call you with a question if I don't know there is a question to call you about." Quinton realized he should have supplied the typist with a list of his symbols. Because of the incorrectly typed symbol, there were corrections on almost every page of the thesis.

Proper equipment is necessary to assure high quality, consistency and accuracy of the final draft. Preferably, the typewriter should have symbol capability. If not, or if some symbols are used that cannot be made by the typewriter, they should be inserted by hand using pen and India ink. Use a template if one is available to assure uniformity and clarity of the symbols.

*Foreign language.* If your paper is written in a language other than English, or contains substantial portions in another language, finding the right typist can contribute greatly to the speed and accuracy with which the manuscript can be finalized. The ideal would be to find a typist who is familiar with the language, but this is not always possible. If the typist is not familiar with the language, typing will probably be on a letter-by-letter basis, without word recognition. This is extremely slow and may delay your time frame as well as result in a high error rate, and the typist would not be able to effectively proofread the work.

Whether or not your typist is familiar with the foreign language, you must provide a clean typed draft. Since a typist transcribes what is seen, your final paper will be as accurate as your draft. Handwritten copy should not be submitted to the typist, because even handwriting that is beautiful to look at may be difficult to read, and is another potential source of errors.

Felicia's thesis was a field study which included reproducing lengthy quotations from Spanish-speaking interviewees. She delivered a heavily spotted, "dirty" photocopy. Even though the typist knew some Spanish, she warned Felicia she was not confident in her ability to know where to place accents, and many of the spots and dots on the photocopy could be mistaken for accent marks. The student agreed to take that responsibility, rather than take time to make another photocopy. As it turned out, because of the time and tedious nature of correcting accent marks, the cost for corrections was greater than the cost of making a clean photocopy would have been.

Equipment must also be considered. Foreign languages can require accents, tildes, umlauts, and other symbols not used in English. A typewriter with symbol capability can produce a crisper final copy than would be possible if the marks were inserted by hand.

Italics have been used in manuscripts to emphasize the portions containing foreign language. If you are considering using italics, check first with the graduate office of your university. Some universities will not accept that typeface. Then check with your typist. If an italic typeface in the language you are using is not available for the typewriter, it may not be technically feasible. For example, the accents on the IBM symbol element will not align correctly with the italic type faces, so typing Spanish in italics does not produce an acceptable appearance. Foreign language elements are available in Spanish, French and other languages, but not in italic typeface.

The amount of foreign language in your thesis will affect whether you need to search for a typist with the ability to understand it. A foreign language typist would not be needed if the thesis only contains a few isolated words or phrases, but lengthy insertions or frequently-used phrases would require a typist with special skills in foreign language.

*Fine arts.* The fine arts are another area in which special skills are needed for typing. It is hard to conceive of a master's or doctoral-level manuscript that would not contain either an analysis of the topic or an original work. Even though "speaking the language" is not so critical as it is in foreign language typing, the typist must have a good eye for spatial relationships, as well as having graphic skills and equipment.

The text in music manuscripts is frequently interrupted by musical notes and portions of scores. Because they are closely interwoven with the text, it is an advantage to have a graphically-oriented typist who can draw the figures.

Art manuscripts contain visuals ranging from simple line drawings to full-page photographs, frequently with a high degree of interaction between the text and the visuals.

Sybil had just completed the coursework required for her master of arts degree. She was a sculptor, and her paper required an interwoven text/photograph sequence. First, the color photographs of her sculptures needed to be enlarged and mounted to near 8 ½ x 11 inches. Her university then required labeling each with the name of the work, her name, year, and a short interpretive description of each sculpture. The whole paper consisted of text presentation and mounted photograph, followed by interpretation, including breaks for chapters and continuations. The typist was familiar with technical typing and photo mounting. Because Sybil's draft was well planned and she worked closely with her typist to ensure correct text, photo, and interpretation sequence throughout, her final product was an effective representation of her growth from her first sculpture and interpretation to her final work.

Scripts in drama require a specific format which is very different from formats required for academic papers. The typing progress would be much more rapid if the typist were already familiar with the style for typing scripts, rather than having to learn it in time to meet your deadline.

## Finding a Special Needs Typist

Hire a typist with graphic and/or technical skills if your work requires it. If you are in a field that requires special typing expertise, the best place to start looking is to ask your professors and other students for a recommendation. The department secretary may maintain a list of typists who have worked for students in the department before. The university's typist list would be a second choice in this case, as the lists do not usually show areas of expertise.

Once you have obtained some names of typists, ask all the questions suggested in Chapter 7 ("You and Your Typist"). In addition, be sure to clearly outline the scope of your work: "I have a chemistry paper, about 75 pages long. Forty of the pages contain equations or chemical structures." Then, if the typist has experience in your field, ask if the typewriter has a half-space ratchet (for equations) and symbol capability. If drawing is needed, find out if the typist is able to do it. Continuing with the example of a chemistry paper, pen and India ink and a chemistry template would be needed to draw in the structures.

After you have determined whether the typist is competent to do the work, ask about time and price. Technical typing is more expensive than standard text typing, because of the level of training needed and the tedious nature of the work. It also takes longer. The other factor that affects time is that, while it is possible to sit and type straight text for eight hours or so, it is not possible to type equations [accurately] for more than two to four hours at a stretch. If your paper is heavily mathematical, it may take more than double the time to type than would a paper of the same length in straight text. You must allow for the increased time/cost elements in making your time line and budgeting your finances.

In selecting a typist, it is up to you to know what your needs are, and search for the best person to do the work. If you need graphics, find a typist with graphics capability; if you need equations, find a statistical or technical typist; if you have foreign language, find a typist familiar with your language, or at least experienced in foreign language typing. Sometimes you cannot meet all your needs with one person, but careful planning will produce good results.

Tom had completed an archaeological dig in Mexico and was preparing his thesis in Spanish. His typist was familiar with Spanish, but was not able to draw the artifacts from his photographs, or reproduce line drawings of maps for his paper. He scouted around and found another technical typist who was also a graphic artist, but was unfamiliar with foreign language typing.

Tom split the work, taking the text to one typist and the illustrations to the other. He planned the draft well, and was able to show his text typist where the artist's drawings would be placed throughout the text. The quality of his final product was excellent, and it was completed well in advance of his deadline.

The writer's responsibility for preparing a very clean rough draft must be stressed again, as well as the need for the writer to proofread all technical material before and after it is typed.

## Dos and Don'ts

Do:

Secure the services of a technical typist for papers with statistical, scientific, foreign language, or other special needs.

Secure the services of a graphic artist for drawings.

Prepare an accurate draft for your technical typist to work from.

Be consistent in the use of numbers and units of measurement throughout your paper.

Provide extra time for your technical typist to work on your paper.

Expect to be charged more for technical typing.

Accept full responsibility for proofreading.

Don't:

Secure a typist unfamiliar with technical, graphic and/or foreign language typing requirements.

Handwrite any part of your draft for your typist to work from in a language other than English.

Presume that your typist can proof the final copy if it is in a language other than English.

## Copying and Printing

In case you are unfamiliar with graphic jargon and print shops, there is a difference between copying and printing. Your thesis may have special needs that require one or the other, so this section is intended to help familiarize you with the world of printing.

*Printing.* Offset printing is a type of reproduction in which the image from the original, or "master," is transferred photographically to a paper or metal printing plate. The printing press transfers ink from this plate to a rubber-surfaced sheet clamped around a cylinder, which then transfers the image from the plate to paper. The transfer of ink is called offsetting.

A print shop's platemaker is an overgrown camera. The quality of your original is therefore very important, because the platemaker will reproduce what it sees. The ideal original will have good contrast — very dark characters on very white opaque paper.

If your original needs to be reduced (or enlarged) to fit your university's margin requirements, this can be accomplished at the same time as the plate is made. Caution must be exercised to make sure the proportional changes in height and width do not affect the perspective or scale to which the drawing was made.

Offset printing produces the highest quality product, although it is more expensive. Some printers have a minimum run (say, 100 copies), which you will be charged for even if you don't require that many copies. Find out complete pricing information before you leave the work. There is sometimes an extra charge for making the plate. You must also make sure the printing paper used will conform to the university regulations, as well as matching any paper used for the rest of the text.

*Copying.* Copying refers to machine copy reproduction or photocopying. In recent years photocopy quality has advanced to nearly match the image of offset press reproduction. Photocopy machines are now available that have color, reduction and enlargement capabilities.

The photocopy method does have limitations. For example, bluegrid or graph paper cannot be used for your master copy because the lines will reproduce. On a pasteup master, a feathering effect may reveal the lines where a pasteup has been adhered to paper. These can usually be eliminated by the machine operator pressing the original very firmly onto the glass plate while taking the photocopy. If this does not work an ink eraser carefully brushed over the lines will usually eliminate them. Or, use white-out correction fluid to eliminate the lines you don't want to show. Then use the cleaned-up photocopy as a master to make the other copies.

Copying has an advantage over printing in that you pay a higher price per copy, but pay only for the number of copies you receive. For a limited number of copies the total price will be lower.

Remember to specify the paper quality to be used for the copies. If only part of the thesis is being copied (the figures or tables, for example), be sure the paper matches the paper the text was typed on. It may be safest to take your own paper, and find a good quality photocopy machine that will use customer stock.

Call several copy or print shops ahead of time to see which meet your needs. Your university graduate office may have a list of reputable copy shops with high-quality machines, and your typist will probably be familiar with the various print shops in the area.

## *Dos and Don'ts*

Do:

Print enough sheets for each copy of your thesis.

Use blue-lined grid background if necessary to formulate a table, figure, or drawing (the blue will *not* reproduce with offset method).

Use black India ink and white opaque paper.

Keep the degree of darkness/density of your original as consistent as possible.

Use rubber cement, waxer, or graphic spray for pasteups.

Use uniform typestyle and consistent quality type.

Use white liquid correction fluid for corrections.

Check to see that your layout/design is as clean as possible.

Hire a technical/graphic typist to prepare your masters unless you are certain you have the expertise and experience.

Use the same paper for your offset copies as you've used for text.

Don't:

Use pencil, ballpoint, or felt pens.

Use tracing paper, onionskin, or thin paper for your originals.

Allow dirt to get onto your original (the camera photographs exactly what it sees).

Allow rubber cement or other adhesives to bleed to the edges of the pasteup original where it can collect dirt (which will photocopy).

Use scotch, transparent, or masking tape to hold items on your paper (photographs and/or blurs images).

Use staples on your original (staple holes show as black
dots on printed material).

## Conclusion

Every thesis or dissertation needs a skilled typist. Many
manuscripts need special technical, language or graphic skills and
experience to give professional quality to the work. The quality of
your visuals can also make or break your thesis or dissertation.
Visuals command much more attention and have a more powerful
impact than text, so poorly-prepared visuals can detract severely
from an otherwise high-quality paper. On the other hand, well-
prepared visuals can help salvage a borderline manuscript.

It may cost more money to have an expert assist in preparation
of your document, but the end results will be well worth the investment. You will have a finished product that is visually attractive,
professional looking, and eyecatching — one you can be proud of!

Chapter 11

# Stress

Students in graduate programs, particularly those juggling work, school and family life, find their lives become much more stressful as their research process gets under way. Learning to deal with the added stress is extremely important if you are to get the most out of your graduate program. Although the suggestions made in this chapter are not intended to be medical recommendations, they are common sense methods of turning negative energy (stress) into positive output.

Stress was called "the rate of wear and tear on the body" by Dr. Hans Selye, the founding father of stress research ("Stress: Can We Cope?," *Time*, June 6, 1983, pp. 48-54). Other researchers use the term to refer to "any external stimulus that causes wear and tear, or to the resulting internal damage." Whatever the accepted definition, stress is part of the package you sign up for when you enroll in graduate school.

Although the effect of stress on health and well-being has been established, researchers propose different causes for it. Psychiatrist Thomas Holmes (University of Washington) determined that "the single common denominator for stress is the necessity of significant change in the life pattern of the individual." In contrast, Richard Lazarus (psychologist, University of California at Berkeley) thinks that the everyday annoyances of life contribute more to illness and depression than do major life changes.

However, as pointed out by Leonard Pearlin (psychiatrist, University of California at San Francisco), both these factors can work together when a single event causes changes that affect daily life. Dr. Pearlin's example was divorce, a major life change that affects day-to-day living because it "is accompanied by some social isolation, a reduction in income and sometimes the problems of

143

being a single parent." In this context, going to graduate school could also be seen as a major life change, with corresponding influence on daily life.

One of the conclusions of the *Time* article cited previously is that stress scholars are convinced that "far more important than the trials and tribulations in one's life is how one deals with them." A number of personal factors were pointed out that seem to be helpful in coping with stress: the sense of being in control of one's life, having a network of friends or family to provide "social support," and having personality factors such as flexibility and hopefulness.

Methods for handling stress vary, with some being more effective for certain types of people than others. Hospitals offer common-sense advice to stress patients: "quit smoking, lose weight, cut down on salt and caffeine, take vacations regularly and exercise." Medication, biofeedback, and muscle relaxation have also been shown to enhance relaxation in some people. While one person may need counseling, another may need only to get regular exercise and vacations.

Acknowledging that you are placing increased demands on yourself and that you will be subjected to increased stress while in graduate school, here are some general suggestions to help you stay in control and stay healthy. (Specific problem areas for students—family and friends, job, money—are discussed in the following chapters.)

## Self-Study

When embarking on your graduate work, you need to do some self-analysis. How do you operate most efficiently? How can you set realistic goals? What are your limits? Knowing something about yourself will help you make the choices that are right for you. Do you like setting up columns of numbers that add up correctly? Is besting the computer a challenge? Do unstructured classroom settings make you nervous? Are you bored stiff by library research? The courses you take and the program you're in are previews of the "real world" in your field. If it doesn't feel right in school, it may not be right on the outside, either.

Answering questions such as these will also help you realize maximum productivity without over-extending yourself. That, in turn, will keep you from being frustrated because of expecting more than is reasonable. If you think well of yourself and accept your own strengths and weaknesses, each day will provide reinforcement and a measure of your progress toward your objective. Even if you take longer overall to complete your tasks, you *will* be able to complete them eventually. It will allow you to attain your goals and measure your successes.

## General Health and Vices

In the interests of maintaining good health, use moderation in pursuing your vices. Smoking, drinking to excess, and overeating all can be detrimental to your health. And take the time to get a checkup if you need it (or someone else thinks you do).

Eat the right foods, and eat regularly. Have at least one hot, balanced meal a day, preferably sitting down and not studying while you're eating it. And stay away from the cup of coffee and candy bar routine instead of meals! In general, restrict your consumption of caffeine-laden foods such as coffee, tea, and cola drinks.

Be sure you get enough rest, and even develop the habit of taking a nap if you feel tired. The amount of sleep required depends on your own body—some people require 10 hours a night while others function well on five. But get a good night's sleep at least four nights a week.

Exercise is important to everyone's body, but particularly to someone who has a heavy, sedentary workload. You can walk, jog, lift weights, bicycle, swim, follow a morning exercise program on television, or do yoga. It doesn't matter what type of exercise you get, so long as you enjoy it and/or are committed to doing it to the point of perspiration several times a week.

## Relaxation

It's OK to take time off from your work—whether for a vacation, small trips with your family/friends on weekends, or a night at the movies with your friends. You must continue to have relaxation, to make time for the extracurricular activities you enjoy. A good way to do that is with other people.

If you can't or don't want to "get away," it's still important to set aside some quiet time for yourself every day. You need this time to get back in touch with yourself, and to get a break from the hectic routine and many demands placed on you.

Ingrid felt pressure from having to complete her dissertation before a fast-approaching deadline. Once it was ready to be typed she turned it over to her typist and left for vacation. She provided a telephone number where she could be reached, took a copy of the rough draft with her in case problems arose during the typing and really enjoyed her vacation. When Ingrid returned from vacation, she was relaxed, her energy was restored, and her dissertation was ready for submission to the university.

## Attitude

"Look on the bright side" and "every cloud has a silver lining" are time-worn expressions you may have grown tired of hearing. But they have hung around because they're true. If you can find some positive aspect to every negative incident, you can learn to work with the setbacks and benefit from them. A professor who sends back your third "final" draft with notations to "now look at it another way," is not trying to sabotage your efforts to graduate. He or she may see your research as a learning process — which it is — and feel duty-bound to give you as many opportunities for growth as possible before you set off on your own in the professional world. You can either become immobilized by your own resentment, or you can accept the challenge and proceed from there. The basic requirement is that you have faith in yourself.

Felicity was taking a course from a well-respected but very demanding professor. He handed out criticism freely on every paper she wrote, and seemed to find no redeeming feature in any of her efforts. She started heading for the candy machine immediately after class. Many pounds and several agonizing weeks later, when the quarter was finally over, Felicity was shocked to receive an A in the course. She asked the professor why, and was told, "I know I was rough on you, but I knew you could take it. You have a lot of talent." [If Felicity had consulted with the professor earlier, or with other students in the program, she would have understood why he was so strict — and saved herself a lot of worry.]

## Anticipate Changes

Changes will be necessary in your plans, your time schedule, and possibly your graduation date. If you expect some changes you will not be caught off guard when they happen. If you don't expect changes, and they occur, you could be devastated and lose valuable productive energy. If changes are required that you do not like but cannot do anything about, accept them and work within the new requirements. Trying to fight it, both in actuality or mentally, will wear you out and will only prove to be counter-productive.

Rachel was not coping with the stress of going to graduate school, working, and running a household. As she entered the dissertation-writing stage she was already taking out her problems on those around her. But the worst pressure came when her husband was transferred to a different state before she had final approval of her dissertation. Since Rachel had always received excellent grades on graduate papers, she was expecting her committee to approve the dissertation without requesting major revision. However, they requested that numerous sections be rewritten. She submitted a second time and was directed to approach the topic from a new perspective. On the third submission Rachel was asked to rewrite large portions of each chapter.

As each draft came back unsigned, the pressure within Rachel built higher. She blamed her husband for the problems because his transfer caused her to leave the vicinity of the university, making communication with her committee members more difficult. She began taking her frustrations out on those around her (husband, friends, co-workers). On the fourth submission, Rachel finally obtained the required signatures, but by that time her marriage was foundering, she had received two reprimands from her supervisor at work, and her relations with friends were strained. [Had she been more realistic in her expectations, Rachel's life would not have taken such a negative turn, and her graduate experience would have been more rewarding.]

## Support Groups

Group discussions/rap sessions are a useful way of dealing with stress resulting from graduate work. Forming a group of students in your graduate program is highly recommended, because they share the common bonds of going through the program together and studying in related fields. Group discussions help you to release your thoughts, frustrations, and fears among people who are sharing common experiences; their input can help you resolve problems. Even if you can't find resolutions, just letting off steam with someone who understands can relieve the pressure.

Sal wanted to form a discussion group with other students going through his master's program. Eight interested students formed a group, and met twice a month. It proved to be a valuable learning/sharing experience for all who participated, in addition to offering a chance to relieve tension by talking about problems. The students found their peers could offer valuable insight and suggestions for resolving conflict. After graduating, several of the students stayed in contact with each other; a couple of them even went into business together. The friendships formed at the rap sessions became a part of their personal/professional lives.

Other sources of emotional support can be found in friends, family, church, and social organizations. Even though people not in school may not have the same immediate problems you do, they might have had similar ones in the past. Or they might have a clearer perspective that could benefit you. It is helpful to have someone to talk to about personal matters, to share affection with, and just to count on when you need them.

If you have a problem and feel you haven't *anyone* to turn to, consider calling your typist. Because of the wide range of people your typist has worked with, he or she might be able to put you in contact with someone who successfully resolved a problem similar to yours. The typist may be able to help you deal with a cumbersome university regulation, or suggest methods of handling unusual format requirements. If nothing else, typists can listen, offer encouragement and let you know that others have experienced similar blocks, changes in schedules, and other setbacks, and they weathered the storm and eventually graduated.

Finally, a word of caution: In looking for people to confide in, be careful whom you talk to and what you say. Expressing your frustration at the barriers you are having to cross is natural; but don't do it in such a way that you are attacking anyone. Present problems and seek suggestions, rather than venting anger at a human target. Remember, seek what *you* can do to assist your graduation process, not prevent it from progressing.

## Conclusion

Stress is part of the package when you sign up for graduate study. A little pressure is a great motivator. But some students find it extremely difficult to deal with the pressures encountered in their schooling, while others seem to take it in stride. Observing the suggestions made in this chapter can help you handle stress, to keep it at a reasonable level so it does not become destructive. The guidelines presented here are simple and beneficial. Essentially, taking care of yourself *physically* and preparing yourself *emotionally* are the best positive ways to deal with the stresses you will encounter.

## Dos and Don'ts

Do:

Eat properly and regularly.
Determine the amount of rest you need and get it.
Exercise regularly.
Analyze yourself and determine what goals are realistic for you.
Anticipate changes and rework your schedule to accommodate them.
Watch for build-up of stress and release it in positive ways.
Take time off from your busy schedule to recreate, vacation, maintain friendships.
Utilize group discussion/rap sessions to verbalize your frustrations and get feedback on what to do.

Don't:

Snack between meals (unless it's fresh fruits and vegetables), or skip meals.
Choose a form of exercise that is unenjoyable to you.
Fight change — work within it.
Think of change as failure.
Take your stress out on others.

Chapter 12

# The Returning Student

Re-entry is the process of returning to college in mid-life or later, after a long absence from the classroom. Today's college population has a rapidly growing number of re-entry students competing actively with typical 20-year-old college students. Why is returning to college so popular now? There are five major groups of re-entry students: (1) displaced homemakers, (2) men seeking a career change at mid-life, (3) women with low-paying jobs, (4) recently divorced men and women who are building new lifestyles, and (5) people forced to retrain because of economic crisis or a changing job market. Many returning students have experienced a combination of these circumstances.

Veronica, 45, worked as a secretary after she graduated from college. When she married and began raising a family she stayed home rather than trying to balance child-raising and a career. After her children were grown, financial pressures forced her to return to work. However, Veronica now found her secretarial skills out of date, so she returned to college to retrain for today's job market.

Lyndon, 55, worked as a business executive for 30 years, steadily climbing the corporate ladder and becoming increasingly financially secure. However, when he reached his 50s he realized his health was being affected by the pressure from his work, and began to feel the need for a more rewarding job. Lyndon returned to college to get a teaching credential. He felt his later years would be better spent training young minds rather than chasing after corporate contracts.

Fran, 35, was a homemaker and mother of three children. When she divorced, she realized she would have to work to support herself and her children. Fran returned to college to train for a profession that paid a decent wage.

As these instances show, there is a wide range of reasons for re-entry into college. Returning students must face multiple new situations and unanticipated changes in their lives, both on a family and a personal level. It can be an extremely frightening experience as well as an infinitely rewarding one. This chapter will deal with the things to expect from re-entry and some ways to cope.

## Effect on the Family

The first major area to look at when considering re-entry is the *family unit*. If you are married and/or have children, what effect will re-entry have on your spouse and/or children? If you are a homemaker, you will have to consider how you will redistribute the household chores (cooking, cleaning, washing clothes, shopping, running errands, etc.). Obviously you will have time to do *some* of your normal tasks, but if you take two classes and also budget time spent on homework, approximately 16 hours of your week will be occupied by school-related activities. Will your husband and/or children share the burden of assuming some of your household chores?

Blanche realized it was important for her own stability to re-gain some sense of herself as an individual, rather than being just someone's wife and someone's mother. She entered the master's program at the local university. Her husband's attitude was, "Whatever you do with your time is OK, so long as supper's on the table when I get home." Her children were at first supportive of their mother as a student, but when she was no longer as available to meet their needs, they became actively resentful. Blanche almost dropped out of school, but then remembered why she had re-entered in the first place. She called a family conference to emphasize how important school was to her, and insisted on cooperation from her family. [It took a lot of effort and bending, but in the long run all the members of the family benefited from being more active participants in running the household.]

In the case of re-entry males (especially where the wife does not work), the family will have to adjust to having the head of household gone/occupied more than usual. If you attend night school two nights a week and study the other three nights, your wife and children can expect to see more of your head bent over textbooks than of your active participation in family events.

It is recommended that any decision to re-enter college be made with active participation of the whole family. If everyone understands *why* you are going back to college, and is supportive of your decision, then a joint effort will be made by all family members to cooperate whenever necessary. (Surprisingly for many parents, children are proud of their parents' school efforts and willingly help out when they understand and are a part of parental decisions.)

Carter was working on a degree in journalism, and spent many late nights working on the university's newspaper. His wife had worked her way through graduate school and was very supportive, but he began to have problems with the two children. Since there was little extra time to spend with them, he decided to take them with him one night. He was pleasantly surprised to see his nine-year-old son prove to be a valuable "gofer" for trips to the cafeteria for coffee and sandwiches, and carrying instructions and prints back and forth between the pasteup room and darkroom. His teenaged daughter, who worked on her high school newspaper, carried back to her school information on techniques used at the university level. She gained a new regard for her father as a student. Carter's only complaint about the otherwise successful experiment was that it took some time before the other students — all considerably younger than he — stopped calling him "dad."

If you reach a point where things seem to be falling apart, chores are not getting done, etc. then it is time for another family conference to remind everyone why a little extra is being required of them and to hear everyone's thoughts. These airing-out sessions can give you valuable insight into possible changes to make and also will revitalize the family effort. (For more on family/adult student situations see Chapter 13, "You and Your Family and Friends.")

## Are You the Teacher?

One of the hardest things for returning students to recover is the *confidence* that they can succeed in school and compete successfully with younger students. They feel that the young students have no worries, no responsibilities, no cares except to do well in school. That may once have been true. But in today's world, many younger students have families of their own to support, are making ends meet by working either full or part time, or they are surviving on student loans or the G.I. Bill. It may be true that they have not been away from school for many years, so their study skills may be sharper than yours; however, they may be suffering from a poorer high school education base than you had.

As an older student, you may feel alienated, not part of the academic community. Having family and job commitments contributes to this feeling as well as being in a different age group than most of the students around you. Don't let this stop you from participating in the extracurricular activities at school — clubs, service organizations, social interest groups, lectures, seminars, elective field trips. These out-of-class activities and the personal interchange they stimulate are as much a part of the learning process as the time spent in class. And you do have something to contribute!

You may encounter some negative feedback. After all, you're "taking up the space" needed for a younger student or one who is going to "repay the scholastic debt" by going into the work force. A handy response these days is that colleges and universities need all the tuition-paying, *qualified* bodies they can get. Teachers also sometimes feel threatened by returning students, who don't hold them in awe, but regard them as another living person with flaws and failings.

After the younger students quit mistaking you for the teacher, and after the teachers stop feeling threatened by your greater years and practical experience, you can begin learning and sharing from each other.

Arriving for her first statistics class, thoroughly frightened of a new topic and certain of failure, Beatrice discovered the professor was an extremely shy person her own age. The professor enjoyed having someone "from his era" in this entry-level class, and Beatrice soon became the anchor student. ("Do *you* understand this?") The other students perceived the difficulty she was having and the professor's concern, and the result was a class camaraderie and sharing from which everyone benefited.

Returning students share the common factor of being at a crisis point in their lives. After making the decision to return to college they are faced with the prospect of seeing all those smiling young faces — a constant reminder of age differences. But for many re-entry students, age simply slips into the background after they begin *succeeding* in college. Suddenly they are competing with and sometimes beating the youngsters. They find the "kids" admire them for what they are doing. Grandparents who return to college find they are the center of attention. Each time newspapers display pictures of a graduating 65-year-old grandparent, holding the hard-won diploma, standing next to his/her grandchild, also holding a diploma, tears glisten and cheers rise. That grandparent has fulfilled the American dream — you are never to old to learn or succeed! All it takes is your determination and effort!

## Time Factor

Every re-entry student needs to make a careful evaluation of time limits and demands on his/her time. Involved here are three things: (1) school time required (including homework), (2) household duties, (3) work requirements (if you are employed either full or part time). One key to success in college is *not* taking on more commitments than you can handle. If you spread yourself too thin you will do poorly on all fronts and feel like you are failing. If you have considerable obligations besides school, maybe you should start with just one or two classes. Returning to school is going to make tremendous changes in your life, so it may be best to try it cautiously at first and let yourself adapt.

One of the adaptations you must make is regaining lost study skills. Many re-entry students have simply forgotten how to take notes, one of the main tools of successful education. Even if you have an orderly home/work life, the school routine is completely different. You must learn to cope in the sterile, unreal world of academia. You may have counted yourself lucky if you had a whole hour of uninterrrupted reading time before returning to school, and may find that is the limit of your productive study time. It will take effort to train yourself to sit and read or study during a two-hour or three-hour break between classes, or to get up at 5 a.m. and study for two hours while the house is quiet. Since only about one-third of the hours devoted to school are spent in class, it is up to you to discipline yourself to find and make productive use of the rest of the time you need.

## Finances

Financial problems are often the cause of a decision to return to school, and these problems usually do not disappear until you have your diploma in hand and are working. If you are a re-entry student with children to support, seek out your university's financial aids office. You may be eligible for federally-funded grants, loans, or work study programs. If you are a good student you may be eligible for scholarships. Some universities have scholarships that go unused simply because students did not apply for them. Find out! Even small scholarship awards can pay the price of your books/fees for a year. Every little bit helps when you are going to school. (See Chapter 15, "Grants and Other Sources of Funding," for more details.)

If you want to work part time while attending college, check with your university's placement office. There are a variety of jobs listed, and you could find something that fits your particular skills/schedule. Check these listings regularly until you find something that appeals to you.

## Support System

Because re-entry is a major force in colleges today, universities usually have a wide range of services available to returning students. If your university has a particularly large portion of students in the "middle-age and above" category, these services will be extensive. Make use of them. They can range from offering pre-enrollment counseling and referral to special orientation, peer group counseling, financial aid counseling, workshops, special courses, and social events for re-entry students. Special offices like the veterans and financial aids offices can also supply support to re-entry students. Some universities will waive entrance exams and allow you to enter on a probationary basis, based on your academic records and/or work history. Ask for complete information on all services provided to returning students.

Utilizing these special programs can put you in contact with other re-entry students, allowing you to form relationships with people experiencing situations similar to your own. Interaction with other returning students can provide a source of reinforcement, counseling, and mutual sharing of the highs and lows of returning to college—in essence, access to a wealth of invaluable exchange.

One final example of a re-entry student will sum up the challenge faced by returning adults, and will also stress the rewards of college education at "mid-life."

Adele, 45, had been an elementary teacher for 20 years when she decided to return to college to complete her master's degree. She continued teaching second grade, and attended late afternoon and evening classes. When Adele began her master's program she was used to communicating and thinking at the second-grade level. Her writing had simple sentence structure, spelling and punctuation errors—it was easily apparent that she was an elementary teacher who had been away from adult-level education for many years. As Adele progressed in the program she grew confident in her ability, became much more skilled at writing, and began developing academically at a geometric rate. By the time she was ready to write her thesis she was a "full-fledged" master's student in all respects. Her friends and colleagues commented about the difference in her, both professionally and socially, and were astonished that it appeared to be the result of her return to school. Adele knew the reward had been well worth the struggle.

## Conclusion

The decision to return to school may be one of the most important decisions you will make in your middle years. It will be both challenging and extremely rewarding if you prepare for it and utilize all the resources available to you. University personnel are aware of the unique adjustments re-entry students must make, as well as the frustrations they will encounter. Trained personnel and support programs exist to help students cope with their special needs. It is up to you to ask questions and actively seek the support you require. If you take advantage of these special programs, you can get moral support that will help you stick to and complete your studies. Your rewards will be more confidence, success, intellectual stimulation, and better preparation for today's job market.

## Dos and Don'ts

Do:

Expect re-entry to drastically change your life, and plan for those changes in advance.

Discuss re-entry with all family members and seek support and cooperation for your efforts.

Divide your responsibilities for household chores with other family members so the burden will not fall solely on you.

Hold family councils so there is time set aside to express thoughts and to reach understandings.

Try hard to regain lost confidence and study skills.

Realize you *can* compete successfully with younger students if you apply yourself.

Explore financial and other support systems offered through your university.

Check to see if you are eligible for scholarships.

Expect to grow via your re-entry experience.

DON'T:

Over-extend yourself — especially in the beginning of your re-entry.

Feel negative about being an "older" student — look around you, you aren't the only one.

Be afraid to seek help and ask questions.

Worry about making life changes in "mid to late" life — many people today are doing it.

Expect re-entry to be an easy process — you will have to work at it.

## Chapter 13

# You and Your Family and Friends

So you've decided to go (or go back) to school. Great! Your family is excited (the kids tell their friends you're going to be a "doctor" or a "master" — what's that?). At first your spouse may be full of warm enthusiasm and support, and your kids will be proud you're in school too. ("Can we do our homework together?")

After the novelty wears off, the testing period begins — your communication patterns with your family and their real feelings about your enrollment in graduate school materialize. You're busy, crabby, distracted, and the money's running out. You're never home when your spouse needs your help most with the kids. The kids think you're an ogre hiding behind a book or, even worse, they think your books are more important than they are. And you're getting worn down, feeling guilty, and wondering whether it's worth it.

Of course it is!

Undertaking a graduate course of study when you have a family must be a family decision. It's a family commitment — treat it as a family project. You must maintain a close relationship at all costs, balancing your workload and your personal needs. How do you and your family reschedule your lives to meet everyone's personal needs, in addition to coping with the burdens of graduate work? Can you continue having a meaningful relationship with your spouse/children so they don't feel unwanted and left out? *You* must make the effort to continue developing your personal relationships to keep a necessary part of your life from being cut off.

By going to school, you are taking time away from family members and reducing or postponing a higher standard of living, making an investment in the future. But your family has to be involved in your decision, too. Aside from the financial aspect, there are some very real emotional questions that arise. The first one involves your spouse.

## *Husband/Wife Relationship*

Married graduate students, whether their spouses work outside the home or not, may find that they are operating on a different intellectual level from their spouses. The student will be taking intensive specialized courses the mate is not exposed to, and meeting people who are involved in the same field of study. After a time the spouse may start to feel left behind — socially inferior, unable to live up to the school-bound spouse's expectations, or unable to compete with students or professionals in the field who may provide a more stimulating environment. The stories of the new doctor or lawyer divorcing his outgrown wife after finishing residency or internship are all too common; and there are plenty of cases of newly-educated women divorcing (or being divorced by) outgrown husbands. These tales prey on the mind of the non-school-bound spouse.

Similarly, a husband's college degree is no guarantee that he will not be threatened by his wife's advancement to (or beyond) his educational level. The same is true if the husband has no formal higher education, and is employed in a manual or crafts-oriented profession. With the wife's increased education comes the potential for greater earnings and job status than the husband has achieved. Although the number of couples in this situation is increasing, some men could be expected to have difficulty coping with it. The student will have to carefully analyze how the spouse is reacting to the change in lifestyle during the graduate program, as well as to the potential for change afterward.

The problem may not be that one partner is in graduate school and the other isn't, so much as that one partner is growing and the other isn't. If the spouse reads extensively or is actively involved in an interest that requires mental energy, the level of stimulation may be equivalent, although the credentials and formal certificates may not be. Thus the partnership will not be unbalanced.

Roberta became involved with a fireman who held a bachelor's degree, while she was working on her master's. Their friends foretold of doom, but this relationship has lasted and grown. The important factor here is not only that the fireman received his education and *then* chose to enter his profession, but that he continued a self-education program and read extensively for his own enjoyment. They never run out of things to talk about.

The fears and problems can be alleviated to some degree by the student's attitude and outlook. If you regard going to graduate school as a regular job, your spouse may regard it as less threatening. If you include your spouse in extracurricular school activities, talk about your coursework, and introduce him or her to your academic associates, the whole academic world won't be a mystery. Encourage your spouse to further his/her education, too. It doesn't have to be at the university level. Special interest and adult education classes are offered on a regular basis in many communities. If your spouse takes some courses or pursues other self-development, he/she will have some inkling of the demands on you for study time. What has become your everyday world must be made real to your spouse if you are to get the communication, understanding and support *from each other* that you *both* need.

Sid's wife, Nellie, started out helping her husband by typing his papers. Then his friends' papers. Then his professors' papers. She now has a thriving typing service with as much business as she can handle, and has a real feeling of what deadlines are and what the students are going through. Nellie plans to turn her cottage industry into an outside business when Sid finishes his degree program and their children are older. She doesn't feel threatened by her husband's academic growth — typing the papers has kept her "in touch" with research being done in a variety of fields, thus allowing her to continue her education without returning to school.

In contrast, another young woman subtly sabotaged her college-bound boyfriend by arranging "special" things for them to do together when he was supposed to be studying or going to class. Rather than put her efforts into keeping up with him, she tried instead to hold him back.

It is extremely important that couples discuss openly and honestly the effects pursuing a graduate degree will have on them. It will make both partners aware of anxieties each has, in addition to allowing them to become alert to the danger areas they need to monitor. There are many success stories about marriages that made it with one spouse going to school. There are also tales of those that don't make it. School by itself will not be the determining factor of whether or not a family or marriage makes it. But it may be the catalyst to bring all the other factors into the foreground. Working together and communicating can help to alleviate fears about the stability of the relationship.

Hillary decided to return to graduate school after being away from college for many years. She did not discuss her decision in detail with her husband, nor did she try to discover if he felt comfortable with her decision — she simply felt he would adapt. Since his education ended at the high school level, he felt threatened by her return to school. When Hillary completed her degree and got a job in the field of law he felt that she no longer cared for her "craftsman" husband. He felt out of place going to her social activities, did not feel comfortable with her professional friends, and felt degraded that Hillary now made more money than he did. By the time he voiced his feelings, it was too late — they ended up divorcing. [Communication was sadly lacking in this marriage.]

Todd worked on a master's degree with the full emotional and financial support of his wife. They talked for hours of what he would do when he got out of school, and planned a future full of monetary rewards that would compensate for the years of scrimping while Todd was in graduate school. Unfortunately the liberal arts degree he obtained did not train him for a specific job, and when he applied for high-salary jobs in areas related to his studies he was deemed less qualified than people with a degree in a specific field. Todd was unable to find the high-status, high-pay job he and his wife had looked forward to. Unable to cope with this failure, the marriage finally dissolved. [Since Todd's main reason for pursuing a master's degree was job placement, he should have sought career counseling before choosing his field of study.]

## Children

Children pose special attention problems. If you are always busy or distracted, or don't get home until after they are in bed (and therefore go for a week at a time without seeing them), they'll begin to wonder who you are, and if you love them. It means the children are getting the full brunt of one stressed parent, rather than a working counterbalancing between both parents. These problems are not restricted to married couples with one partner in school. They are common to more and more households — single parents, one or both parents in a high-stress and demanding job, even swing and graveyard shifts can produce problems in children who may be lead by TV or school books to think that what's going on in your family is not *normal*.

You must work to maintain your relationship with your children. Children (especially young ones) may not fully understand what you are doing when pursuing an education, and why. Your activities with your children, and their active involvement in your graduate work, will depend to a certain extent on the age of your children, but you must communicate with them and *create* time for them. Make some rituals. Show up for story time. Eat lunch with them. Be a part of their lives!

*Young children.* If you have young children (under school age) you must remember to maintain a routine that includes some time with them. If a family excursion usually occupies Saturday afternoon (trip to the park, rowing on the lake, movie) continue that practice. Children look forward to such outings and if you stop them or they are carried on without your presence, young children may feel you are either unreliable or you don't care. The continuity of a family outing with *all* members participating is extremely important to kids. In fact, if you had not developed such a routine, it might be wise to start one now, since you will not be available at other times.

Arthur knew that the amount of time he spent going to classes, studying and completing his research would greatly detract from the hours he spent with his family. He and his wife agreed that, no matter what, Sunday would be a day for the family. They planned inexpensive outings and all family members participated. The children realized that even if they saw little of "daddy" all week long, they would have him for the whole day on Sunday. Arthur made an effort to have the children understand all about his graduate work. He took them to the college campus, he introduced them to some of his fellow students, he had his committee members over for dinner so the family could meet them. The children felt that they were a part of their father's graduate process and were satisfied that they were contributing their share.

*Older children.* If your children are school age they will be able to understand the ideas behind why you are going back to school, and should be active participants in your discussions on the subject. Older children will probably be called upon to contribute more to household chores (especially if the spouse is also returning to school or to work), and they should be aware of *why* these changes in the home are taking place. Confide in them and let them contribute their ideas. They will feel a part of the family program and can take pride in your achievements because they helped by doing their part. (For more details see "Running Your Household" later in this chapter.)

Franklin wanted to return to school but felt uncomfortable asking his wife to support the family. He knew the additional education was necessary to advance at his job and believed the family would prosper from his decision in the long run. Franklin discussed his feelings with his wife and learned she was willing to be the breadwinner while he was in school. They decided the financial drain on their savings would be worth the reward at the end. They requested the support of the children — in understanding their parents' decision, in taking on more household chores, and in doing babysitting and odd jobs in the neighborhood to provide for their entertainment money (since their allowances would be cut). The entire family backed the father's decision — so he went to school. Everyone made the necessary sacrifices and offered whole-hearted support while Franklin completed his degree.

## Involving Your Family

No matter what the ages of your children, there is one extremely important point to remember — *kids have needs that must be filled whether or not you are a student*. Don't ignore your children's needs and don't ignore your children. Allow them to participate in your school activities where appropriate. Many campuses have functions where children are welcome; they may show movies or sponsor festivals, and most universities have sporting events that all family members might enjoy. These activities serve the purpose of making the school more a part of the community. If you include your children in school activities, it will make them feel more a part of your life, too.

A side benefit to this is that it may develop some special talent in your spouse or children.

Tyler's graduate biology project became a family adventure. The children, after a couple of weekend visits to the animal lab, became avid assistant caretakers, very willingly cleaning cages and doling out food. Tyler's wife was involved in the excruciatingly tedious task of assisting in tallying and keeping records of weights, breeding histories, and animal marking.

This may be an exceptional case, but it needn't be! It's only an example of what is possible. Take your family with you to the music recital, to the computer lab, to the department picnic, on the weekend field trips (one eight-year-old daughter on an ecology field trip was the star sample-finder, possibly because she was closer to the ground).

Crystal was taking an art class, which alternated a lecture section and a laboratory section where the students worked with different art media. She talked to the instructor, and while they agreed it would not be appropriate for Crystal's nine-year-old daughter to come to the lecture section, she was welcome in the laboratory section "as long as she works like everyone else." The daughter worked side-by-side with her mother, and produced beautiful artwork which was displayed along with the work of other students in the class.

If you have library work to do, you might try taking your family with you on a weekend. Some university libraries have a children's section. On a pretty day, there may be a grassy knoll ideal for a picnic or throwing a frisby. Activities such as these depend on the atmosphere and regulations of your university. The attitude and acceptance of children on campus varies greatly and may be determined by the number of students who have families. There usually is an easing of restraint in this area as the school year progresses and students get more settled into and comfortable with the academic environment. Also, as more students with families go back to school, the universities are getting accustomed to seeing children on campus as active participants.

A word of caution is in order, though. Except in announced special circumstances, the classroom is no place for children. No infant is "quiet." They gurgle and make other noises distracting to students who aren't familiar with them. The smell of dirty diapers in a closed classroom can be unbearable. Even older children are not capable of sitting absolutely still and listening with rapt attention to a lecturer, no matter how interesting the topic. While it is important to include your children in your education as much as possible, do not do it at the expense of the other students in your classes.

Make the extra effort (even when you don't feel you have the time) to allow your children to feel wanted, loved and cared for. You might have to delay your graduation a quarter in order to spend a little extra time with your kids, but you will still graduate. Your children will only be young once—and they are growing up while you are in school. If you forget about them, their childhood is lost to you; you cannot turn the years back to recapture what you have lost with your children. If you make a concentrated effort to involve your family in your academic career, they will feel a part of it and proud of you; equally important, you will win their true support!

Olivia completed her college degree and received her teacher's credential just before marrying. Her husband, Ned, was a doctoral student. He discouraged her from working after a miscarriage. She then became a housewife, bearing four children. Ned worked and completed his doctorate, then became an assistant professor at a university and got involved in department politics. He kept his family totally separate from his profession. He began, in essence, "hiding" his rural wife and their four children from his fast-paced, urban-oriented university associates. It was not until Ned applied for a divorce several years later that he took the time to learn that Olivia had become a highly respected counselor in her church, and had applied for and been approved as qualified to teach their children at home. She had also been accepted into graduate school. Ned realized too late that he did not need to throw away his family when he grew — they were capable of growing with or without him.

## Running Your Household

Now what about your part in running the household? How are the household jobs distributed? This is a time of true communication and sharing. Or frustration! Make a list of the family jobs (everything from making out the shopping list to mowing the lawn to doing the laundry). Take a look at who has been doing each job, and decide who will do it now. It may be worth it to let the intricate landscaping go and hire the kid down the street to mow the lawn once a week. Or maybe you like to do the yard work for relaxation and would be more willing to give up some other chore. Dividing the chores (with a minimum of conflict) is possible with communication and setting priorities. Also remember: It's one thing to support your spouse in school, and another thing to support your spouse in school so long as nothing around the house changes. *There are going to be changes*, face that! Go back to your list and decide who's going to do what, and stick to it for a specified amount of time. Then revise the list if necessary. Remember, the jobs that have been yours to do in the past must either be done by you now, delegated to someone else, or put off to some future date (like quarter break). One family made each family member responsible for maintaining their own laundry—from washing and folding clothes to ironing and sewing on buttons. It didn't take very many days of wearing "relatively clean" clothes to school before the kids caught on that their parents were serious and no one was going to do their laundry but themselves!

This is a good time to involve the children more. Turn over the lawn to the oldest child. An amazingly young child can push a vacuum cleaner and dust furniture. It may be worth it to make a weekly run to the laundromat to get the laundry all done at once (you can read during the wash and dry cycles), instead of doing it at home a load at a time. Any job that has to be done takes time and thought, no matter how small it is. Many that are done routinely now must be reevaluated to see (1) if they need to be done, (2) if *you* still need to do them, (3) if they can be broken down into parts and wholly or partially delegated. Kids can set and clear the table. You can clean up after yourself if you come in late. You can keep your books and papers in a concentrated location to (1) minimize destruction possibilities by family, and (2) minimize the housekeeping clutter that will get to be greater as you get busier.

Your own attitude will in good measure determine the response you get from your family. Don't use school as an excuse to not get something done or to not spend time with your family. Ask yourself if you would do whatever it is, or spend time with whomever it is, if you weren't in school. Are you going to school because you have the goal of an advanced degree, or are you staying in school because you're reluctant to leave that environment and get out into the "real world"? You have to ask and answer all these questions. Your family's survival as a unit will depend on how you handle the answers, and how well you know yourself and your own motives.

Finally, don't forget that many universities offer counseling services for students and their families. These services are provided at a reduced cost or, in some cases, free. You've paid for the use of facilities in your student fees. Take advantage of them!

## Time for Study

If you're making an effort to keep the family unit together and working smoothly, you won't get attacks of guilt when you need quiet time and have to shut the door. It helps if you have a regular place to study. You need a desk and a place to keep your stuff. It can be in the corner of the bedroom, in a study, or in an office at school.

As you have to establish times to spend with your family, you must also establish times to be away from them. They must understand that there are times when you must not be disturbed. You may not look like you're doing anything if you're reading, but that's your job now! Again, it's up to you to enforce the privacy rules. If you allow your family members to come knocking on the door, disturbing you during that period, you're defeating your own purpose. Make sure your spouse is in agreement with your chosen work times — it doesn't set a very good example if your spouse is allowed to knock on the door and interrrupt you. If your spouse takes your academic commitment seriously, this will be transmitted to your children.

## Money

You don't need to be told that many graduate students suffer from money problems, especially if they have a spouse and/or children. Students find diverse ways of handling these problems; among them are:

1. working full time and going to school part time or at night;
2. going to school full time and working part time;
3. taking out a loan;
4. having your spouse share in or shoulder the burden of financial responsibility for the period of time covering graduate school;
5. applying for alternate sources of funding (grants, graduate assistantships, etc.) (see Chapter 15, "Grants and Other Sources of Funding");
6. having parents or other relatives aid in education expenses.

In most cases there is a period of sacrifice and drastic cutting of expenses, so if you are going through that, remember you are not alone.

Why, then, have you been reading about all the activities you should engage in with your family? Activities cost money! True. But the ones suggested here are low cost or free: picnics, visiting animal labs, going to the university library or computer center, attending department family functions, spending a day at the park, meeting your classmates.... You can and will find ways of spending time together without straining your budget, if you try.

## *Roommates*

The problems of spousal relationships also apply to some extent to roommates. If you are rooming with a friend who is going to school as well, your roommate will have a basic understanding of your needs and requirements because they are common ones. You and your roommate can achieve a successful rooming partnership, based on consideration of each other's needs, even though you are not engaged in a long-term relationship. If your roommate is not going to school, you may encounter different problems. Simple things that may not have been of consequence earlier, now assume paramount importance. Your needs for quiet study time may conflict with your roommate's desires to play the TV or stereo, or to have friends over. Your increased load at school may lead to your not keeping up with your half of the housekeeping chores. Your time commitments may be greater, so you can't engage in spontaneous activities as often. Or your roommate may not like your new friends from school. You may be able to resolve the quiet problem by staying at school to do your studying in the library, so when you do come home the noise level won't be a problem. With some effort you can probably resolve the other problems, too. Or you may decide to look for another roommate whose activities would present less of a conflict.

## *Friends*

Friendships are formed and hang together because of mutual interests, experiences, and feelings. But friends do not need to be clones of each other. Differences can contribute to and enrich a relationship. A new interest or activity does take time and energy, and the person with the new interest is going to meet other people engaged in that activity. How well the older, established relationship weathers this period will depend on how well founded it is on a broad base of interests and mutual respect. You have probably encountered a "drifting away" of friends before, as your interests diverged or you simply grew away from each other. Look back over the past 20 years — were you in the "in" group or the "out" group when the topic of the year was encounter groups, the peace movement, women's liberation, jogging, reborn Christianity, or home computers?

Now it's your turn to take off in a new direction. You've thought it through and decided it's right for you. You will make some new friends during the course of your graduate experience, and some of your older friends will realize it's part of the growing and learning in life, and it's something you have to do. Others may feel threatened or left behind. Don't let the responses of your "friends" determine or alter your resolve. The friendships that survive your graduate degree will be all the stronger for it.

Friends—both old ones and new friends met through your graduate program—can be extremely helpful support groups. Spend time with them. Use them as a soundingboard for talk about your work. But don't forget to listen, too. You can get ideas from them and also learn information about problems they are experiencing. In such a relaxed atmosphere you can gain insight as well as unwind. This is extremely important for someone balancing work, school and family, and is an excellent source of positive energy.

Marcie had a solid network of friends who were not involved in the field she was pursuing in her graduate work. She met several new friends in her master's program. She felt close to both groups and realized she would like to integrate them into one group in order not to lose either set of friends. Marcie gave a party with both groups attending, hoping they would like each other and form an enlarged circle. She had guessed right! The qualities she sought in friends were a part of both groups. Although their professional pursuits were different, they quickly realized they enjoyed each other's company and shared mutual recreational interests. Marcie was able to consolidate both groups of people into one strong support system.

## Conclusion

Your family and friends will provide an enormous support system for you during your graduate years. They will help you cope with the added stress in your life—but only if you let them. You will have to make the effort to communicate with them, seek out their support and active participation. Their degree of involvement will depend on your ability and desire to solicit your aid. The importance of these relationships to graduate students is easily illustrated: browse through the dedication and acknowledgment pages of several theses/dissertations. Who is listed and why?

I dedicate this research in memory of my late mother, who taught that the best way to better myself was through education.

I want to express my deepest appreciation to my husband and two children who encouraged me to continue my education, even though it meant time away from them.

Special acknowledgment is made of the invaluable support I received from Tom and Julie, my best friends — without their constant prodding I would never have reached the end of my dream.

The list is as endless as the encouragement and support graduate students receive from family and friends.


## Dos and Don'ts

Do:

Strive to understand your husband's/wife's feelings about your graduate work.

Realize your marital life will undergo many changes, and be willing to work to make them positive shifts.

Monitor your own feelings toward your graduate work, inspecting the changes forced on you.

Determine the level at which your children should be a part of your graduate process, and keep them informed/involved appropriately.

Spend relaxing hours with all family members (including vacations and weekend trips).

Communicate your thoughts and feelings freely and encourage your family and friends to do so too.

Recognize that your children have needs that must be met — and meet them!

Utilize the family conference method whenever it is appropriate.

Organize your time.

Set aside uninterrupted time for yourself.

Utilize counseling services available through the university, if needed.

Keep relationships with friends active.

Integrate new and old friends whenever possible.

Value your family members and friends — they will be a tremendous support to you.

DON'T:

Take family members and friends for granted.

Expect family and friends to understand what you are
going through — you must tell them.

Waste time!

Take your stress out on others.

Forget … your children are growing even while you are in
school — you mustn't lose those years.

Let your family or friends sabotage your efforts.

## Chapter 14
# You and Your Job

A large portion of students attending graduate school are holding down a full- or part-time job. Whether you need or want to work (or already have a job you want to keep) will depend on your individual financial situation. Taking your family restraints, location and job requirements into consideration, there are several alternatives to consider: Should you go to school full time and work part time? How about going to school part time and working full time? Can you support yourself on loans and grants and complete your education more quickly or with less stress? Assuming you will be working, give serious thought to how much time you can spend at school and on the job. Temper that with how much money you need to meet basic living expenses. Adding one class to a full work day is manageable, but a schedule that allows class time for three classes and then adds work hours to total 40 hours a week is unreasonable, and will only result in wearing you down rapidly. You must allow time for travel between school and work, and for other needs essential to your survival — sleeping, eating, family, and studying.

The following discussion of options starts at one end of the scale and works toward the other. Any of the work/school arrangements discussed can prove beneficial to your needs; however, we do not consider full-time work/full-time school as a viable alternative.

## Full-time Employment

Full-time employment with school can work in several ways:
- 9 to 5 job combined with night school;
- 9 to 5 job with release time for classes;
  - variable schedule job (such as swing/graveyard or split shift) with daytime classes;

•alternative work hours (7-4, 10-6) with early morning or evening classes.

The bulk of class offerings is in the middle of the day, but many universities start classes as early as 7 a.m. and continue until 10 p.m. At some schools (particularly those with a high percentage of employed students), it is possible to complete an entire graduate program without setting foot on campus in the daytime.

If your job is unrelated to your degree program, or if your firm offers its own training program, your employer may be relatively unsympathetic to your scheduling needs. You and your supervisor or personnel officer must determine this. Even though not encouraged by your company, your advanced degree may qualify you for a new line of work within the company; or you may need to leave the firm and search for new employment. Thus, holding a full-time job unrelated to your academic interests is the least advantageous option — you are not guaranteed advancement with the firm, your contacts may not be effective in your new field, your working experience may not be contributing to your education, and your employer may be unsympathetic to the extra demands on you.

Blanche had worked full time in a clerical position since obtaining her liberal arts degree. When she decided to return to graduate school, she spoke to her employer about release time for classes. Her employer refused, saying if she wanted advancement in the firm she should apply for their management trainee program. They did not feel an advanced degree in her field would be of benefit to the firm. Blanche decided to keep her job and go to night school for the first year, and then search for a part-time job while she completed her degree.

Warner had a college degree which qualified him as a technician. When he reached the top of his category, he inquired about further chances for advancement. He was told he had gone as high as he could go in his job. Privately, he was told that while the company could not subsidize his further training, if he showed the determination and initiative to seek it on his own, he would be qualified for another line of work within the company, with greater advancement potential. Warner took the chance.

If your degree program can in some way be related to your present employment, and if you have been a stable and productive employee, your firm might be willing to contribute to your efforts. Some of the benefits companies offer workers who go to graduate school are:

1. flexible work hours (arrive late, leave early, long lunches);
2. release time to attend classes;
3. payment of fees;
4. reimbursement for expenses;
5. secretarial services for typing papers (or payment of private typist fees);
6. study time for major exams;
7. study time for major research projects;
8. financing the thesis/dissertation if the project results will help the company;
9. promotion at the completion of the degree.

Here's how it works:

Rodney was working full time when he decided to go for his Ph.D. His company agreed to allow him to work half time while he completed coursework and wrote the dissertation. The company paid all educational expenses and guaranteed him a position in management when he finished his education.

Before approaching your employer to discuss your plans, answer the following questions:

1. How many hours a week can I work and still do quality school work?

2. What support would I like my employers to provide (release time, payment of school fees, payment of textbooks, thesis typing costs)?

3. If the company is willing to assist me, what will they get in return?

4. Can I design a research project that will directly benefit my employers?

Once you have determined what you would like your company to offer, decide whether or not you can tailor your graduate work to fit the needs of the company. What problem areas does the company experience? Can you design an experiment that will shed some light on solving those problems (i.e., graduate work in business, computer science)? Are you picking up expertise that will help the company in the future (i.e., design, communications, mathematics, statistics)?

Once you have given these areas some serious thought, check into your company's policy on educational benefits. Many large corporations have well-developed programs for employees, while others simply need you to present your plan. If your company has guidelines to follow, pursue them. If not, draw up a written proposal outlining what you plan to do and why, what you would like the company to provide, and how the company will benefit from this educational program. Submit your plan to your supervisor or personnel director and follow through until you get a decision.

Jessica was a business major who attended classes at night, so she did not need release time from work. Her thesis was an analysis of a problem the company was experiencing. She designed a project that described and analyzed different ways the company could try to solve its problem and presented solid recommendations. Since the project was company-related, they paid for her fees, books and thesis typing. Both Jessica and the company profited from the experience.

One word of caution: If you make an agreement with your company, abide by it and don't take advantage of your employer. If your supervisor offers to allow you time off to attend a 4:00 class on Monday and Wednesday, don't take off on Tuesday and Thursday also. If they agree to pay for books and fees, don't charge them for classes unrelated to the degree (if you are a business major, you could reasonably expect payment for courses in computer usage or statistics, but not sociology or art). And if your employer tells you he will assist you for a three-year period, but at the end of that time you must have the degree — expect that he means it!

Guy took a full-time job after completing his graduate course work, but before finishing his dissertation. He could keep his job for only two years before the degree had to be conferred. When Guy began the job, he did not realize the amount of time the dissertation would consume, nor did he anticipate the number of changes and problems that would come up in completing it. As time began to run out, his employer reminded Guy of their agreement. He ended up barely making the deadline for the dissertation — the typist finished only minutes before the dissertation was rushed to the airport. The deadline was met and he continued in his job, but Guy spent considerable time overcoming the side effects from the extreme pressure he had been under.

## Leave of Absence

If you can afford it, you might want to consider taking a leave of absence from work to complete an educational program. The positive sides to this are being able to complete the work in a shorter period of time and being able to concentrate solely on your academic endeavor. Check to see if your company has a policy on leave of absence; if so, follow the guidelines. If not, any request for a leave should be made in writing to your supervisor, stating the reason for the request, the length of time you would like off, and the benefit to the company.

Tracy was married shortly before she decided to go to graduate school, so could afford to take a leave of absence from her job. (Her husband was willing to be sole breadwinner while she was working on her master's degree.) The company Tracy worked for granted her a leave of absence for two years to complete her coursework, and agreed to let her come back part time for two years while she completed her thesis, because the project was related to the company. At the end of the four-year period she was guaranteed a full-time job with promotion and substantial salary increase.

## Part-time Employment

Part-time employment has advantages over full-time, provided you can meet your financial needs with the reduced income. Working fewer hours gives you the time necessary for classes and study, without incurring the obligation to "pay back" an employer. If your employment is related to your field of study, you still have the option of increasing to full time after you have finished school.

Another way to approach employment while in graduate school is to get a part-time job totally unrelated to your academic career. This approach has been popular and successful with students who have a high-stress or mentally taxing area of study. While income is necessary, a job which stops when you walk out the door and requires little mental or emotional commitment does not dissipate the mental energy you need to get through school. A few examples are: pumping gas, grocery or store clerking, driving a hearse, working in a bookstore, house-sitting. While these may not promise permanent employment, you never know:

Ida was a skilled typist, so decided to try supporting her graduate studies by typing for students and faculty. As her reputation grew, her typing load increased to more than she could handle and still keep up with her studies. She hired another typist to help, and then another. When Ida finished her master's, she studied her options and decided to put all her efforts into development and expansion of her cottage industry, which has now become a successful publishing business.

Another option is to find work on campus—in the cafeteria, bookstore, library, an office, or a research lab. You might be able to find a job in your department, which would have the added benefit of giving on-the-job practical training. An obvious advantage of working on campus is elimination of travel time and expense, and the possibility of greater flexibility in blending work and class time. Understandably, there is a lot of competition for on-campus jobs.

## Graduate Assistantships/Fellowships

If you have no means of financial support and your academic record is good, you might consider applying for a graduate assistantship from your academic department. These funds are not abundant, but many universities have a *limited* amount of money to partially support some of their graduate students. These funds are usually dispersed based on academic records and financial need, and the requirements vary from university to university. If you are interested in applying for a graduate assistantship, teaching assistantship, or fellowship, contact your department office. The financial aids office will have information about funds available to students for scholarships, loans, and grants. (See Chapter 15, "Grants and Other Sources of Funding.")

## Internships

Your department or the career counselor at your university may have an arrangement with the business community whereby advanced students work as interns for a specific period of time. Internships are professional apprenticeships—opportunities to work in your field under the direction and guidance of employed professionals. It is a sample of the real world your academic career is preparing you for. The duration may be for a term or a year, or for a specific project. It may be for pay, for academic credit, or both. Internships are mentioned only briefly here, because they are rare and do not provide continuous income. But they provide invaluable experience and contacts, and many result in permanent employment.

*Conclusion*

If you need income from working while going to graduate school, study the options. Determine how much time you need for school, study, family and travel, as well as how much money you will need. Find a full- or part-time job that will best fit your needs for time, income and training. There are many school/work combinations that can be productive and rewarding.

If you are working when you make the decision to go to graduate school, you may have an available source for financing your studies — your current employer. Spend time organizing your proposal, make it fit the needs of the company, and consider what benefits you would like your employer to offer. If you succeed in obtaining financial assistance from your employer, you will become an even more valuable employee. Even if your company has no history of helping college-bound employees, don't let that discourage you — maybe no one has asked for it.

*Dos and Don'ts*

Do:

Be realistic when planning the amount of time you can spend working and studying.

Analyze what you would like from the company and put it in writing.

Use your education to produce something of value to the company.

Fulfill any agreement you make with your company.

Check at the university for alternate financing if you have no job.

Investigate part-time jobs unrelated to your field.

Don't:

Undertake so much that you do a poor job at work and school.

Expect the company to pay for your education without any benefit to them.

Expect your job to be there if you don't fulfill your agreement.

Overlook any source of employment — look at how a job may fit your needs.

Chapter 15

# Grants and Other
# Sources of Funding

One of the questions that can influence whether you go on to graduate school (or return to it) is where to get the money to pay for it. The question can arise again when the process turns out to be more expensive than you had foreseen, thus using up your resources faster than you anticipated. Up-front costs of tuition, lab fees and books can be calculated with reasonable accuracy, but variable quarter-by-quarter transportation and other living costs can be harder to estimate, especially if your tenure in graduate school takes longer than you planned.

Likewise, if you considered the cost of typing your thesis at all, you may not have figured in the cost of having it grow from 100 to 200 pages, of having it typed twice or more because of committee revisions, or of finding out that doing it yourself on the kitchen table wasn't adequate.

Graduate school is expensive, and you also need money for living expenses while in school. If you have a spouse who is working and earning enough to support you completely during graduate school, or if you have parents who are able to do so, you're fortunate. An alternative to the working spouse/parents option is for you to supplement the family income with a part-time job. Or, you can continue working full time while going to school. (These topics are discussed in Chapter 14, "You and Your Job.")

Each of these options assumes going to school while working, or having someone support you. These arrangements are certainly workable and have been used for many years, although they do place an added emotional/psychological stress on you and those around you, in addition to the financial ones. The people involved must recognize that this arrangement, simple though it sounds in the beginning, is going to go on for several years and will put a hardship on the living unit. (See Chapter 13, "You and Your Family and Friends.") This is not to try to dissuade you from doing it that way. The spouse/family arrangement will work so long as there is clear, open communication among the people involved.

A less emotionally demanding means of support is to seek outside funding sources. These are available in various forms — grants, loans, scholarships, and other benefits. Surprisingly, many sources of funding for graduate study go unclaimed each year because no one applied for them. It will take some legwork and research on your part, but there are many sources available.

In this chapter we have not tried to make a comprehensive list of sources of funding — that would take volumes and be rapidly out of date. Rather, the following material describes the range of funding available and shows where to look for it.

## Types of Funding

Many different terms are used to mean "money for education." For the sake of clarity, here's a summary:

*Scholarships* (also called fellowships, competitions, prizes, awards) are sums of money given to students to pursue their education. They are generally specific as to amount (a fixed dollar amount), purpose (tuition and books), or duration (one, two, three or four years). They are sometimes awarded on a competitive basis, and are usually awarded on the basis of academic merit.

*Grants* are money given with few or no strings attached, based on financial need. Grants can be awarded for general assistance while going to graduate school, or for specific purposes such as covering the cost of typing a thesis or dissertation. A grant is usually applied for, frequently by preparing a proposal, and periodic progress reports are sometimes required.

Scholarship and grant money does not have to be paid back, although payment can be stopped if you drop out of school or otherwise fail to maintain the status for which it was awarded.

*Benefits* are money that comes to you for education because of a service you or your family has rendered in the past. The Veterans Administration, Social Security Administration, and other organizations offer educational benefits to workers or dependents, usually on a fixed time-worked/benefits-earned scale. Since this money was previously earned, it does not have to be paid back, but payments will be stopped if you fail to meet the requirements for receiving them. You are held accountable for any overpayments, and future payments can be withheld until any deficit is cleared.

*Loans* are funds received from any source that has to be paid back. Guaranteed student loans may be the best funding source for students who don't have the grade-point average for a scholarship, and who don't meet the financial need criteria for a grant. ("Guaranteed" because the federal government indemnifies the lender against part or all of any default in repayment.) Some student loans are interest-free, some carry low interest rates, and some have market interest rates, depending on where the money comes from and how long you plan to use it. Methods of paying it back vary from making periodic payments during the course of your schooling, to beginning payments after you graduate, to making a bulk payment at some agreed-upon date.

Before getting into details about the search for money, a cautionary note: Start looking well before you need the money. Your library work and letter writing should start as much as a year before you enter graduate school. (But if you didn't start that early, don't give up before you start—just get moving!) Some funding sources have application deadlines a year before an award is made. Some suffer the cumbersome wheels of bureaucracy or have limited staffing. Others are well known and have many applicants, so you need to give yourself time to apply elsewhere if your application isn't accepted. You can apply for more than one funding source, although some sources won't give an award if you *receive* funds from another source (they prefer to spread the money as widely as it will go). The full grant or scholarship is rare, and even a full one will not support you in the style to which you may like to become accustomed.

Do your research and make applications with confidence that there is money out there for you. In its manual, *Foundation Fundamentals: A Guide for Grantseekers*, The Foundation Center reports that

> 950 of the approximately 22,000 active private foundations are currently making awards directly to individuals. Well over 50 percent of the awards made by these foundations are for educational assistance, including scholarships, fellowships, and loans.

And remember—there's nothing wrong with getting financial assistance while going to graduate school. Even if you don't pay it back in dollars, you pay it back by increasing your contribution as an individual in a working economy.

## Sources of Funding

Since funding comes from so many sources, the most efficient way to start looking for it is geographically. Let's start close to home.

*Local Sources.* As mentioned in Chapter 14, do you have an employer who will cover part of the cost of your school expenses, or who will give you time off (with or without pay) to go to school? If your firm has no such regular program, a well-thought-out and well-written proposal may result in your being the first subsidized student on the payroll. Sometimes the employer will pay for the cost of typing the thesis, especially if it is a research project needed by the company.

Community organizations have full or partial scholarships for college students. Service organizations such as the Rotary clubs have scholarship funds, and other special-interest groups sometimes have funds to support graduate study in their area of interest. Check with your local chamber of commerce and local chapters of professional organizations in your field of study.

Your city may administer a grant-in-aid program, which provides part-time employment for students, loans at reduced interest, or administers bequests from individuals.

If you or your family are members of a church, union or fraternal organization you may be eligible for that organization's scholarship program. If you are the dependent of a deceased member of the organization you may be given special consideration or priority for financial assistance.

Cameron was studying for his Ph.D. in theology. Having a family to support while he was in graduate school made things financially tight. He received support from his parents, his wife's working part time, and backing from congregation fund-raising.

Local businesses sometimes sponsor competitions for scholarships for advanced study in their field.

You may have a family source—a relative or family friend with money who is willing to invest in you. Sometimes there is a tax advantage for the donor to divert some income to a family member with lower income. Your arrangement could be to pay it back when your benefactor is past his or her peak earning years and would pay taxes on it at a lower rate. Be cautious in accepting money in any form from friends and family. For your own peace of mind and to rid you of any assumed "strings," make it a business arrangement, complete with contract and arrangement for repayment.

> Barnaby was working on a master's degree in law. A long-time family friend offered to foot the bill for his education, with the agreement that after his law practice got off the ground he would repay the education costs. [In this case a financially secure older friend willingly invested in the future of someone he considered a "good risk."]

Depending on the population density where you live, sources similar to the ones listed above may exist at the county or regional level. A broad rule of thumb is that locally-oriented funding sources tend to have fewer assets and give either single awards or several small ones. Their staffs are usually smaller and application turn-around time may be longer.

*State Sources.* Many of the sources of funding found at the local level have statewide equivalents. Your state government may have student loans, grants, or scholarships for persons demonstrating ability and need. Special programs are available to help disadvantaged or handicapped persons. You may be eligible for benefits under the state's veterans program, either as a veteran or dependent.

Statewide organizations have scholarship programs to encourage further study in their area of interest. Sometimes they will award a grant for research on a specific problem, or sponsor internships for applied training.

State branches of national organizations may have their own scholarship or loan program. Again, check to see if the state level of any fraternal or professional organization you or your family belong to offers financial assistance for graduate students.

Check with the state assemblyman or senator from your district. Frequently if a scholarship is available the source will contact the elected representatives to see if they can nominate someone. Your representative will also be able to direct you to the right office to inquire about state-sponsored financial assistance.

*National Sources.* At the national level are both nationwide organizations and the various agencies of the federal government. Service and special-interest organizations abound, offering funds on the basis of academic merit, demonstrated need, disadvantages, handicaps, and even lineage (don't forget the Daughters of the

American Revolution). Some offer funds on the basis of financial need or scholastic record, while others are more limited and specify the course of study.

National-level businesses and foundations have scholarship programs, as do the national equivalent of unions and other fraternal organizations. Professional organizations offer scholarships for advanced study in their field of interest. National-level organizations may have more funds at their disposal, and are able to give more or larger grants.

Your senator or congressman's office may be well informed about private as well as public sources of academic funding for advanced study. Like the state representatives, the national elected representatives also receive last-minute calls asking for nominations for an unclaimed scholarship.

The most well-known sources of funding are probably the Veterans Administration and the Social Security Administration. The education benefits of the GI Bill have put many students through school, either earned by their own time in service or as the dependent of a veteran who died or was disabled in military service. Similarly, the Aid to Families with Dependent Children (AFDC) branch of the Social Security Administration provides educational benefits to qualifying dependents.

## Resources

The best is always saved for last. The two most valuable places to look or receive guidance from are right at your fingertips — your own university and the public library.

Your university will probably have a financial aids office. It's probably a very busy place, but there is a lot of information if you take the time to dig through it. The staff will have received notices from funding sources of all kinds, and will also have information on benefits the university provides. The school may have financial aid ranging from on-campus part-time jobs, listings of part-time jobs off campus, housing for students, private scholarships administered by the university, departmental awards for students in specific areas of study, loans, work-study programs, and so forth. Sometimes the university will waive fees for students demonstrating financial hardship. Some universities have a research office as well stocked with reference materials related to funding as your local library, complete with a staff person to guide you through it. Some universities also have a separate veterans affairs office to help arrange financing and handle other questions related to schooling needs. There may be a re-entry office or organization with information on funding specifically for re-entry students.

Check with your department office. Financial assistance may include:

- graduate assistantships — grading papers for faculty members;
- teaching assistantships — teaching lower-division courses (lecture or lab);
- private tutoring;
- research assistantships — working with faculty members on state- or federally-funded projects;
- scholarships;
- internships;
- part-time jobs related to your field of study.

Wilma was working on biology research, under the supervision of two faculty members who received federal grants. Her master's thesis was based on work she performed under their guidance, and much of her expenses were paid by the research assistantship she received from their federally-funded project.

The reference librarian at your local library may turn out to be the best single source of information. The library will have a collection of books listing specific sources of grants, scholarships and loans, complete with mailing addresses of the organizations, requirements and submission deadlines. The skill of the librarian may save you some time in your search by starting you off in the right place.

Here is a representative book list to start with:

Kurzig, Carol M. *Foundation Fundamentals: A Guide for Grantseekers*. New York: The Foundation Center, 1980. This manual explains the process and gives valuable instruction on how to select a private funding source and how to apply.

*Paying for Your Education: A Guide for Adult Learners*. College Publications Board, 1980.

Learner, Craig Alan, and Roland Turner. *The Grants Register, 1983–85*. New York: St. Martin's Press, 1982 (published biannually). Contains comprehensive listing of awards, by subject (cross-coded to applicable area), by name of award and by granting organization.

*Catalog of State Services.* Sacramento, Calif.: Office of Planning and Research, 1976 (published annually). Each state will have an equivalent document. This volume for California lists financial assistance ranging from retraining to aid while going to school.

*Catalog of Federal Domestic Assistance.* Washington, D.C.: Office of Management and Budget, 1981 (published annually). This volume gives details of assistance for education available through the federal government, including the AFDC portion of the Social Security Act, student loans, aid to disadvantaged groups, and assistance in special fields such as medicine and teacher training.

Lewis, Marianna O., exec. editor. *The Foundation Directory,* 8th ed. New York: The Foundation Center, 1981. This index gives (by state) specific foundations, their addresses, donors, purpose, activities, and other financial data. Grants application information and application deadlines are listed.

*Veterans Benefits.* Title 38 – U.S. Code, 92nd Congress, 2nd Session, House committee print #223, December 20, 1972. Washington, D.C.: U.S. Government Printing Office, 1972. This volume contains the letter of the law regarding educational and other benefits for veterans of military service.

*Federal Benefits for Veterans and Dependents.* Washington, D.C.: Veterans Administration, 1981. This volume contains an unofficial but easily understandable summary of the benefits available to veterans as of January 1, 1981.

## Conclusion

This brief survey of funding sources has only been a sampling to show what is available. As with all other aspects of your graduate career, how successful you are at finding outside funding will depend in large part on how thoroughly you do your research and how aggressive you are in pursuing it. Many applications are rejected each year because the applicant's area of study does not fall within the clearly-stated objectives of the granting agency. A lot of wasted time and hope can be spared by carefully screening foundations and agencies, and concentrating on a few well-chosen ones. People will be your greatest source of information – your reference librarian, the staff at your university financial aids office, the staffs of your local government officials, your personal or family contacts. There is no way to avoid spending a few weeks of intensive grant-searching to get the process under way, but the effort will be repaid if you are successful, and have to spend fewer hours at work or worrying about money.

## Dos and Don'ts

Do:

Make use of all resources available to you.
Start looking for money before you need it.
Make sure you only submit applications to appropriate agencies.
Check all available sources of funding.

Don't:

Assume this is a waste of time — many scholarships go unclaimed.
Forget to provide all required information.
Limit your application to just one source.
Be embarrassed about seeking financial assistance.
Feel badly if you don't get an award — you're no worse off than you were if you hadn't tried.

# Chapter 16
# Post-Graduate Slump

After the hustle and bustle of working on a master's/doctoral degree, many students find themselves in a slump once it's over.

There are many different ways the slump hits students: a general malaise — something is wrong but you can't quite put your finger on it; having a nagging feeling that you have something you should be doing but you can't remember what it is; having a tremendous surge of energy you are not used to; having too much time on your hands, allowing yourself to become idle; losing the momentum that was keeping you productive — now you can't get *anything* done; catching a cold; depression!

The depression is clinically documented: Dr. D.W. Sue (*Understanding Abnormal Behavior*, Boston: Houghton Mifflin, 1981) discussed the example of the scholar who is awarded an advanced degree after years of hard work and perseverance, only to feel unhappy and depressed about it instead of elated or joyful. This is "success depression."

J. Mendels (*Concepts of Depression*, New York: Wiley, 1970) examined a number of possible reasons for success depression: Achievement of the goal may bring new demands, requiring greater responsibility and competence. If the person is accustomed to playing a dependent role, it may no longer be possible after the success is achieved. The person may have low self-esteem and not feel worthy of the achievement. Success may produce guilt feelings if the achievement unconsciously symbolizes a competitive feeling toward someone close to the student. And, after achieving a long-sought-after goal, the person may experience an emotional and physical slackening that may produce guilt and depression.

Another explanation for the success depression paradox relates to learned helplessness, described by M.E.P. Seligman (*Helplessness*, San Francisco: Freeman, 1975). Apparently successful

189

people may become depressed because their reputation and recognition are based on previous achievements or on circumstances beyond their control, rather than on present performance. "In the case of the new Ph.D., recognition and respect are now a function of the title rather than the individual's actions.... Much of the increase in depression that clinicians see in today's youth results from a perceived lack of connection between their own efforts and their affluence."

The slump depression can also be related to the fact that you were working under tremendous stress, were juggling many aspects of your life, and had a specific goal. You were organized while working "under the gun" to get your research completed, had little or no spare time, and had many things on your mind at once. Suddenly that is gone!

The best way to avoid such a slump is to keep the graduate work from being an isolated, self-contained part of your life. Don't let your goal-setting stop with the degree! Each phase of your personal plan should overlap with the phases before and after it. For example, if you are finishing a master's degree and want to complete a doctorate, your applications for doctoral programs should start before your master's work is finished. Likewise if you're completing a dissertation and want to do post-doctoral research.

If you're planning to start a business, your marketing studies, advertising strategy and business plans should be started while you're still in school, so all the energy and momentum you will have can be used to build your business.

If you're planning to work for someone else, write your resume, send out letters of inquiry and attend job fairs before you graduate.

The transition from school to post-school can be smooth. Even if you don't have time to do the actual legwork for your next endeavor while in graduate school, you can realize there will be a "next" and do some of the planning.

If you have reached graduation and realize you hadn't planned what to do next, you still needn't sink into a slump. Here are some suggestions:

*Employment.* If you have a job (one you worked at while doing your graduate work, or a new one) you will find most of your daytime occupied. You will probably find your job receives much more of your energy, and the slump won't materialize. If you don't have a job, but plan to work, spend as much time as possible in the pursuit of employment. Organize your resume, write letters to companies, seek interviews, do all the things necessary to get that job. You will find your spare time occupied in the search for employment.

*Set new goals.* The quest to finish your graduate work kept you going for two or more years. Now you need a new goal. It doesn't matter whether it is pursuing further studies, taking up a hobby, planning a family, or developing the habit of reading for pleasure. But set new goals so you can organize yourself around them.

*Continue a rigid exercise routine.* This will help burn up the excess energy released by the reduction in stress and will also occupy your time. It may also allow you to meet new people and broaden your social life.

*Build up an active social life.* This will give you enjoyable leisure time, will allow you to discuss ideas about the future with others, and will occupy some of your spare time.

*Use your graduate research.* Can you publish portions of it in magazines, journals, or newspaper articles? Do you want to extend it and write a book? Can you adapt your teaching lesson plans to meet requirements of your school district, as a handbook for other teachers? Find constructive uses for the work you spent so much time on. This will broaden your horizons professionally, and will allow you to feel your graduate work was valuable and useful.

Following are some examples of how post-graduate slump affected different students.

Holly had taken a leave of absence from her job while she worked on her master's thesis. The week after she finished her degree requirements she was back on the job. She also sought to reactivate her social life so she would not have too much spare time on her hands. Holly realized that being inactive would depress her after being extremely busy for three years. Friends suggested that she should take a vacation for a couple of weeks before going back to work, but her response was "I can do that next summer — I need to be *busy* right now."

Mitchell finished his master's degree in June and was planning on beginning a Ph.D. program in September. He felt he needed the three months between programs to rest and re-energize his system. But after a short time he started feeling depressed. Mitchell ran into his advisor on campus one day and mentioned his depression. The advisor realized he was too inactive. She suggested Mitchell rework sections of his thesis for publication as journal articles. He took her suggestion and found the depression lifting as he became occupied. Mitchell realized he could not cope with being inactive after living under extremely stressful conditions for so long. He also felt satisfied that he would have some articles being considered for publication at the time he started his Ph.D. program.

How you handle post-graduate slump will depend on your lifestyle. You can be creative in evading the slump by acknowledging the possibility of its existence and working to keep it at bay. If you find the slump or depression creeping up on you, take a look at your motivations and feelings about where you have been, where you are going, and why. Professional counseling may be in order, or you may just need to acknowledge and talk about your feelings. *Don't lose sight of why you went to graduate school in the first place* — was it to broaden your future work horizons, to increase your own personal worth, to make more money, to train in a new field, to be competitive in today's job market? Whatever your reason, it was probably *not* simply to finish the degree. At the completion of your education (especially if the degree took many years to obtain) you may feel the degree itself was the goal. It was not! Resurrect your original goals and look at them again — you may get some keen insight into the direction you want your growth to take now. Moving in those directions will alleviate post-graduate slump.

## Dos and Don'ts

Do:

Expect a post-graduate slump if you don't keep occupied after completing your graduate work.

Set new goals to begin working on.

Use up excess energy constructively.

Rebuild an active social life.

Determine ways you can use your graduate research so it has extended meaning.

Pursue new interests.

Don't:

Expect your life to continue productively unless you

reorganize and continue the momentum you had during your graduate work.

Get lethargic.

Say "It can't happen to me."

*Part V. Conclusions*

## Chapter 17

# Conclusions

Now that you know what to expect from your graduate experience, *don't quit!* This book was written to help you get the most out of your graduate years, not to discourage you from pursuing higher education. The instances cited have illustrated both positive and negative experiences. You will not run into all the problems noted, but you will be prepared for those you encounter.

It has been our intent to (1) prepare you for circumstances you may not have expected; (2) show you how to avoid areas of conflict and frustration; (3) encourage you to change things when you can, and be flexible when you can't. We have attempted to teach what questions to ask, when and where to ask them, and whom to seek assistance from. Now use the book as a reference source — refer to chapters as you need help in solving problems and leaping hurdles you encounter in the completion of your graduate degree.

The following themes have been prevalent throughout the chapters:

- plan well, organize your time;
- take stock of yourself, know your strengths and weaknesses;
- ask questions, seek expertise when you need it, and utilize resources available to you (committee, department, university, other students);
- be flexible;
- don't ignore your personal needs (health, family, friends, relaxation);
- be alert for warning signals of things going wrong;
- stay in control, and keep your project moving;
- live up to your agreements;
- don't get discouraged;
- you and only you are responsible for your work.

In attending graduate school you are embarking on a challenging and rewarding experience that will probably open new doors to your future. You should remember *why* you are in graduate school, and be formulating your plans for after you completed your degree. Will you go on for more graduate study? Will you expand your career (either into a new field or promotion within your current company)? Will you publish some of your research (journal articles, teaching aids, magazines/newspaper articles, a book)? How will you pick up the pieces of your life with family/friends? How will you gear yourself up for the new challenges ahead?

Your graduate work will propel you into a period of growth, both intellectual and personal; it should also raise your confidence and marketability. You will have invested so much time, effort, money, blood, sweat and tears in your graduate program that you may feel the desire to insure your thesis/dissertation for $1 million with Lloyds of London—after all you have been through, that amount may seem fair as its replacement value. You are not alone in this feeling, and taking extreme precaution in the final stages of handling the document is warranted, as this final example illustrates.

Joel had many setbacks during the processing of his doctoral dissertation, including a seriously ill faculty member, three major rewrites required by his committee, and moving across country before the dissertation was approved. His job required that the Ph.D. degree be conferred by a certain date, or he would be dismissed. On the last day for submission, Joel worked frantically with his typist on final revisions. When they were done he rushed to the airport, arriving at the plane just minutes before take-off. The package was flown across country, picked up by a taxi driver, and delivered to the university on time. Pre-arranging the taxi pickup and delivery was a precaution that allowed submission of the manuscript in time to meet the deadline.

If you have met all the other graduation requirements and submission of the document is the last step, you may feel you have to resort to extreme measures to protect the final part of your degree program. On the other hand, if you still have courses to complete or comprehensive exams to take, keep up your momentum until everything is finished. Then enjoy the feeling of relief and accomplishment. You will have completed one of the most self-enhancing experiences of your life!

# Appendix A
# Checklist

This checklist will serve as a key to items and steps to complete in your graduate career and in processing your thesis or dissertation. Use it as a helpful guide, not an ironclad list of regulations. The items are listed in the approximate order they will occur, although individual programs will vary somewhat. You may need to add a couple of steps, repeat some steps, or you may be able to combine some.

\_\_\_\_ Read graduate catalog and department handouts
\_\_\_\_ Fulfill any conditions of entrance
\_\_\_\_ Select degree
\_\_\_\_ Plan courses with graduate advisor
\_\_\_\_ Obtain copy of thesis or manuscript guidelines:
    \_\_\_\_ department
    \_\_\_\_ university
    \_\_\_\_ style manual
\_\_\_\_ File forms to declare candidacy for graduate degree
\_\_\_\_ Take comprehensive examination
\_\_\_\_ Select committee chairperson
\_\_\_\_ Select committee members
\_\_\_\_ Select research topic
\_\_\_\_ Write research proposal
\_\_\_\_ Submit research proposal to committee
\_\_\_\_ File signed research contract in department office
\_\_\_\_ Complete courses
\_\_\_\_ Initiate graduation check
\_\_\_\_ File intention to graduate and pay fees
\_\_\_\_ Complete review of related literature
\_\_\_\_ Write chapter on related literature
\_\_\_\_ Compile bibliography/references and put in form required by style manual

____ File necessary forms to graduate (when appropriate; this will vary from university to university, and will depend on how long you expect completion of your thesis/dissertation to take)
____ Test your methodology
____ Collect data
____ Analyze data
____ Write rough draft
____ Revise rough draft
____ Select a typist
____ Submit rough draft to committee members
____ Incorporate committee members' changes
____ Revise rough draft
____ Submit draft to editor if needed
____ Finalize photos, figures, any other special requirements of your thesis/dissertation
____ Obtain initial approval of committee members
____ Submit figures to graphic artist if needed
____ Read edited rough draft for content and legibility
____ Submit rough draft to typist
____ Proofread thesis/dissertation
____ Return thesis/dissertation to typist for corrections
____ Turn corrected thesis/dissertation over to committee members for proofing and signatures
____ Have oral presentation/defense of dissertation
____ Determine that all forms and requirements for graduation have been completed
____ Return thesis/dissertation to typist for changes required by committee members
____ Submit thesis/dissertation to university graduate office
____ File necessary forms (for submission, title change for cover, copyright, binding, etc.)
____ Pay any necessary fees at the graduate office (copyright, binding, etc.)
____ Pick up thesis/dissertation from graduate office and deliver to typist for any changes
____ Make required number of copies
____ Submit original and copies to graduate office for binding
____ Pick up bound thesis/dissertation from graduate office

## Appendix B

# Tips on Preparing Work for Your Typist

(Or, how to keep your typist happy and reduce your typing bill)

### *Organizing/Rough Typing*

- Don't put only one line of a new paragraph at the bottom of a page (a widow) — leave a minimum of two lines.
- Don't carry over only the last line of a paragraph to the top of a page (an orphan) — use at least two lines.
- Make sure your subheadings are in correct place on page, or have arrows showing where they go.
- Don't use contractions (don't = do not; doesn't = does not).
- Divide words correctly according to a dictionary.
- Don't divide words from bottom of one page to the top of another.
- Don't abbreviate words unless you want the typist to abbreviate.
- Mark inserts clearly (1, 2, 3 or A, B, C).
- Indicate exact place in text where inserts go.
- Keep all pages (including inserts) on 8½ x 11" paper.
- Place inserts immediately after the page where they are to go.
- Be consistent in spelling in your rough draft (don't spell it "post-test," "posttest" and "post test").
- If you have handwritten copy, make capital letters obvious.
- Indent paragraphs or indicate by symbol that they are to be indented.
- Indicate where quotations start and end.
- Page number the draft.

199

- Clearly mark what is to be deleted from draft and where typing starts again.
- Don't insist on use of archaic grammatical rules unless it's the topic of your paper.
- Don't use professional titles such as Dr., etc. in your text or bibliography; use only the last name.
- Always give page numbers for exact quotes or paraphrased reference material.
- Don't refer to figures, tables, etc. as "below" or "the following" or "on page ____" — use "(see Figure ____)" or "(Figure ____)."
- Do not use first person ("I have discovered") in your thesis unless you have specific instructions or permission.
- Type or write your draft on one side of the paper only.
- Don't type "wall to wall" for your draft — approximating final margins will give you a better idea how long the final copy will be.
- Make clear corrections by crossing out and retyping, using correction tape or white-out, not by striking over.
- Use a pen with dark ink to write your draft, not pencil.
- If you write your draft in a spiral notebook, tear out the pages and trim the rough edges before you deliver it to your typist.
- Use regular-weight typing paper, not corasible bond or onionskin, for typing your draft.

## References

- Put your bibliography entries in correct order.
- Include all information necessary for the reference: author name and initials; title of chapter/article, title of book/journal; date of publication, city, publisher, for books; page number if an article, volume and issue number of a journal.
- Order reference citations in text by date (1981, 1983), not by importance or other factors.

## Corrections

- Follow your typist's instructions on how to note corrections on the typed draft.
- For word processing drafts, do not cut and paste. Mark all corrections clearly and use arrows and notations to show inserts.

## Lists to Give Your Typist

- Show how you indicate something is to be deleted, moved.
- Difficult-to-spell names and terminology used in your paper.
- How to spell words that could be spelled more than one way (preschool, pre-school).
- List of words that should be hyphenated in text.
- Full, correct spelling for words you have abbreviated in text.
- List of things inconsistent in rough draft, and how you want it typed in final copy.
- List of symbols used in your work, such as "lower case script ell," "lower case sigma," with your notation of the symbol.
- Draft table of contents so your typist can see the ranking of headings and subheadings.

# Index

# P

Paper: computer printouts 124–125; provided by typist 74, 89; quality 22, 101, 104–105, 140; regulations 104; requirements for theses/dissertations 64; *see also* Typing; Typist; University

*Paying for Your Education: A Guide for Adult Learners* 186; *see also* Grant sources

Pearlin, Leonard 143; *see also* Stress

Photographs 43; defined 78; mounting 132, 133–134; photomicrograph legends 121; presentation in theses/dissertations 132–133, 137; reproduction of 131–132, 141; *see also* Graphics; Typing, special skills; Visuals

Photomicrographs 132–133; *see also* Photographs

Pilot study 38

Plates: defined 117; copying of 132; mounting of 132; *see also* Graphics; Typing, special skills; Visuals

Politics: of department/university 18; rivalries 26–28

Post-graduate slump 189–193

Preliminary outline 46

Prerequisites, course planning 7

Printer 104; *see also* Word processing

Printing 118, 139–141

Program planning 5–17; in time line 13, 17

Project *see* Thesis/project

Proofreading 58–61, 67, 77, 86, 87, 99, 101, 104; foreign language 135; visual presentations 120

*Publication Manual of the American Psychological Association*, 2nd ed. *see* APA manual

# Q

Questionnaire(s) 37, 38, 49

# R

Rates for typing 70, 73, 74, 78–82, 85, 97; *see also* Typing; Typist

Rates for word processing 74, 88, 99, 101, 103, 105, 113; *see also* Word processing

Raw data, placement of 48

Re-entry students 150–157; age differences 153–154; family effects 151–152; finances 155; postgraduate slump 189–193; time factors 154; support system 155–156; *see also* Financial aid; Grant sources

References: citing 48–49, 54; research proposal 11; typing 70; writing 46; *see also* Bibliography; Research; Writing

Regulations *see* Department; University

Research 15–16, 18; advisors' responsibility 41–42; design 36, 38; experimental model 37, 39–40; historical analysis 37–38; negative results 41–43; planning of 35–45 (*see also* Program planning); project 26; proposal 11, 17, 36; methods 37–39, 47–48; results of 41–44, 48–49; review previous 36; scientific method 37; statistical and analysis 36, 38, 40–41, 43–44; technical aspects 35–45

Revisions 3, 67, 108–115; avoiding 33, 108; committee requirements for 14, 56–57, 108–111; draft 14 (*see also* Drafts); due to advisor(s) 28, 30–31; editing help 57–58 (*see also* Editing); rates and charges for typing 70, 74, 78–82, 85, 99, 101–102, 105–106, 112–114 (*see also* Typing; Word processing); revising 53–54 (*see also* Revisions); time line plan 12, 15, 61, 111 (*see also* Time line)

Robinson, Arthur, *Elements of Cartography* map presentation 130

Roommates 168

**GTU Library**
2400 Ridge Road
Berkeley, CA 94709
(510) 649-2500